DISCARD

# THIS I
# BELIEVE

## KENTUCKY

Previous books in the This I Believe series:

*This I Believe: The Personal Philosophies of
Remarkable Men and Women* (2006)

*This I Believe II: More Personal Philosophies of
Remarkable Men and Women* (2008)

*Edward R. Murrow's This I Believe:
Selections from the 1950s Radio Series* (2010)

*This I Believe: On Love* (2011)

*This I Believe: On Fatherhood* (2011)

*This I Believe: Life Lessons* (2011)

*This I Believe: On Motherhood* (2012)

# THIS I
# BELIEVE

## KENTUCKY

*Foreword by* Bob Edwards
*Introduction by* Keith L. Runyon
*Edited by* Dan Gediman *and* Mary Jo Gediman

BUTLER
BOOKS

OLDHAM COUNTY PUBLIC LIBRARY
308 YAGER AVENUE
LAGRANGE, KY 40031

Copyright © 2013 by This I Believe, Inc.
All rights reserved.

This I Believe® is a registered trademark of This I Believe, Inc.

Published by:
Butler Books
P.O. Box 7311
Louisville, KY 40257
phone: (502) 897-9393
fax: (502) 897-9797
www.butlerbooks.com

No part of this book may be reproduced or transmitted in
any form or by any means, electronic or mechanical, including
photocopying or recording, or by any information storage
and retrieval system, without permission in writing from the
copyright holders or their assigns. Requests for permission
may be directed to permissions@thisibelieve.org.

Grateful acknowledgment is made to Henry Holt and Company for
permission to reprint Frank X Walker's essay, "Creative Solutions
to Life's Challenges." From *This I Believe: The Personal Philosophies of
Remarkable Men and Women*. Copyright © 2005 by Frank X Walker.
Reprinted with permission from Henry Holt and Company, LLC.

Further acknowledgment is made to John Wiley & Sons for
permission to reprint the following essays: "Important Strangers" by
Leslie Guttman, from *This I Believe: Life Lessons*, copyright © 2011 by
the author; "Dancing to the Music" by Amanda Joseph-Anderson,
from *This I Believe: On Motherhood*, copyright © 2012 by the author;
"A Lesson I Hold Dear" by Kara Gebhart Uhl, from *This I Believe:
Life Lessons*, copyright © 2011 by the author; and "The Power of
Parenthood" by Andrea Coleman, from *This I Believe: On Motherhood*,
copyright © 2012 by the author.

ISBN 978-1-935497-66-0

Library of Congress Control Number: 2013951175

Printed in the United States of America

To Margot Trevor Wheelock,
who was responsible for
This I Believe

# Contents

# Contents

# Contents

# Contents

# Contents

# Contents

# Contents

# *Foreword*

~⌒~

## Bob Edwards

I BELIEVE IN THIS I BELIEVE, A PLATFORM THAT CELEBRATES our most precious freedom. The Founding Fathers secured freedom of speech in our Constitution—but not right away. It came as an amendment to the original document, only to be restricted by the Sedition Act before our young country had even entered the nineteenth century. Again in 1918, Congress made disloyal, profane, or abusive language punishable by up to twenty years in prison if directed against the country, its flag, or its army. This occurred at a time when immigrants, leftists, and labor leaders were regarded as dangerous enemies.

In the 1920s and '30s, Supreme Court Justice Louis

Brandeis became the champion of free speech as we know it today. Brandeis was not afraid to defend the most unpopular opinions—even the view that the government should be overthrown. Brandeis wrote, "Fear of serious injury cannot alone justify suppression of free speech and assembly. Men feared witches and burned women. It is the function of free speech to free men from bondage of irrational fears . . . Those who won our independence by revolution were not cowards. They did not fear political change. They did not exalt order at the cost of liberty."

Brandeis wrote that in 1927. Edward R. Murrow was a teenager then who would become a debater in college, where speech was his major. His first job at CBS was to arrange for speakers to give talks. Murrow was the father of broadcast journalism and called radio "that most satisfying and rewarding instrument." But he also understood that the new tools of radio and television provided opportunity, not authority. He said, "Just because your voice reaches halfway around the world doesn't mean you are any wiser than when it only reached the other end of the bar."

In 1951 Murrow was an executive at CBS, and one of the programs he founded was *This I Believe*, the title coming from a phrase his mother used. It was a time of enormous fear in America and condemnation of anyone who had ever held unpopular leftist opinions. Careers and even lives were destroyed over one's beliefs. People were sent to prison for refusing to name others who held unpopular views. Many of the essays in the original *This I Believe* series concerned that fear. When Murrow addressed it on TV, he said, "We will not walk in fear, one of another. We will not be driven by fear into an age of unreason if we dig deep in our history and our doctrine and remember that we are not descended from fearful men, not from men who feared to write, to speak, to associate, and to defend causes which were for the moment unpopular." Murrow's own outspoken beliefs about broadcasting and its reliance on the commercial dollar cost him his career. Corporate authorities are even less tolerant than the political variety.

Many of the original This I Believe essays were published in several books, and one of the books caught the attention of radio producer Dan Gediman. He revived the series, and more than a hundred thousand essays have been submitted in the past decade. Citizens speaking out. I believe that should endure.

# THIS I
# BELIEVE

## KENTUCKY

# *Introduction*

———❧———

## KEITH RUNYON

FOR THOSE OF US WHO CALL KENTUCKY HOME—WHETHER
by birth or by choice—our commonwealth has a vivid per-
sonality. It's unlike anywhere else. Maybe that's because
Kentucky is 380 miles wide and 140 miles deep. Or perhaps because it's perched right between the North and the
South. Almost certainly it's because our ancestors, for the
most part, were hardy pioneers, people seeking a better life
on a new frontier.

For more than forty years I was privileged to report and
comment on the issues and people of our remarkable state
from a berth at Kentucky's largest newspaper, the *Courier-
Journal*. During that time, I learned something else about

Kentuckians: they can be ornery, narrow-minded, and sometimes downright reactionary in the way they look at issues and at one another. I guess this must be a legacy of the days when duels were all too common (otherwise, why would we be the only state in the Union that requires public office holders to swear they've never fought in one?). Those clear attitudes had a lot to do with the divided nature of Kentucky during the Civil War, when brother quite literally fought against brother and neighbors split on their devotion to the Union or the Confederacy.

Perhaps it is the opportunity to bridge those divides that makes the This I Believe experience so important here in the Bluegrass State. This exercise in aspiration, launched in the early 1950s by CBS newsman Edward R. Murrow and revived a half-century later by Louisville broadcaster Dan Gediman, calls forth the best of its participants, who are asked, in just a few hundred words, to summarize what it is that guides them in life. The results of these efforts are impressive, often inspiring, and almost always memorable.

In this volume, there is an unusual collection of contributors; some of them were original contributors to *This I Believe* in the 1950s. At that time, CBS radio and its Louisville affiliate, WHAS, which broadcast the essays, and the *Courier-Journal*, which published them, helped to unite the state in a way that no longer exists. Literally every citizen could read the same editorials, news stories, and sports scores from Harlan in the southeast to Henderson in the west. Today we're wired together by Internet and websites; even *This I Believe* is part of this new way of gathering information (www.thisibelieve.org).

In addition to these "heritage" pieces, you will find a diverse selection of writings from contemporary contributors, people of all ages, regions, and perspectives. Among them are some of the commonwealth's most notable personalities and writers, which we hope will make this book of interest not only for its ideas but also for the sheer beauty of its prose. And you will also find statements by people you haven't heard of yet—writers and artists, nurses and doctors, educators and students.

Take a moment to read about the beliefs of this diverse group of citizens, and then consider the origins of your own core values—the things that provide the foundation for who you are. Whether it's an "aha" moment, an inspirational person, or the place you call home, we invite you to share your story by penning your own This I Believe essay.

# Learning Where Home Is

◡

## Angela Ward

October 18, 2004: The clouds were thick and gray as I sped southwest down Interstate 64 that fall day. My entire eight-hour trip seemed to be variations on a theme, and unfortunately, the theme was gloom. Carcass-strewn roads; thick, oppressive fogs; desolate, lonely highways—I saw it all that day. But as I passed the Ashland Oil smoke stacks that line the eastern border of Kentucky, an amazing thing happened: the skies cleared up. Blue skies were finally above me, and the sun shone over the entire Kentucky landscape. Green here, autumnal accents of orange and crimson there, the rolling hills of Kentucky stretched before me for miles. And I wept. For release, for relief, for love, I sobbed.

For the first time in my life, I truly believed in Kentucky.

I moved to Pennsylvania in the summer of 2004 to begin my time as an English graduate student after living my entire twenty-four years of life in Lexington, Kentucky. At that time, I was frantic to get away—away from everything—and start my life on my own. I was determined *not* to stay in my hometown for the rest of my life. I had even come to resent Kentucky as an ever-present threat of self-stagnation. So I cut ties with Kentucky and moved away. Yet, now, against all odds, I believe in Kentucky.

I remember summer mornings at Pine Mountain State Park in southeastern Kentucky, where my family vacationed when I was young. The atmosphere was always heavy and calm with the still-resting mountain clouds; croaking frogs and drilling woodpeckers were the only sounds to greet me as I breathed deeply of air tinged with the earthy, slightly bitter scent of fallen beechnuts. I remember forging my way through the glossy green leaves and pinkish-white blossoms of rhododendrons to the top of the mountain where blueberries—the mountain's treasures—awaited me.

When I took time off from school after college, my job required a thirty-minute commute to a small town called Midway. I remember taking the winding back roads to work, simply so I could pass through the scenic horse country that radiates out from Lexington on all sides. I would meander down narrow roads, bordered on both sides by Kentucky's trademark limestone fences, a canopy of sturdy sycamore and hickory trees filtering the sun so that the asphalt below me was charged with glittering, golden movement.

These are the scenes that pass through my mind now when I think about Kentucky. But it took me time to appreciate them, to really believe they had any power.

I've learned a lot in my twenty-eight years. I've learned that growing up is hard, really hard. I've learned that love doesn't always last, even when you want to think it will. I've learned that I'll sometimes be lonely and that I'll often feel out of place.

But I've also learned that I'm never out of place in Kentucky. I've learned that, aside from my loved ones who live there, Kentucky itself holds power for me. Slowly, I've been able to build a home for Kentucky within me, but Kentucky has always been more generous. Although it took me a while to realize it, I now know that Kentucky always did and always will offer me a home. Welcoming me back no matter how long I stay away, Kentucky gives me comfort, solace, a sense of belonging. And for this, I believe in Kentucky.

ANGELA WARD *currently lives in State College, Pennsylvania, where she is a restaurant manager. She graduated from University of Kentucky before earning her MA in English from Pennsylvania State University. She composed this essay while teaching there—when she asked her students to write This I Believe essays for an assignment, they challenged her to do the same.*

# I Am Still "The Greatest"

~

## MUHAMMAD ALI

I HAVE ALWAYS BELIEVED IN MYSELF, EVEN AS A YOUNG CHILD growing up in Louisville, Kentucky. My parents instilled a sense of pride and confidence in me, and taught me and my brother that we could be the best at anything. I must have believed them because I remember being the neighborhood marble champion and challenging my neighborhood buddies to see who could jump the tallest hedges or run a foot race the length of the block. Of course I knew when I made the challenge that I would win. I never even thought of losing.

In high school I boasted weekly—if not daily—that one day I was going to be the heavyweight champion of the

8

world. As part of my boxing training, I would run down Fourth Street in downtown Louisville, darting in and out of local shops, taking just enough time to tell them I was training for the Olympics and I was going to win a gold medal. And when I came back home, I was going to turn pro and become the world heavyweight champion in boxing. I never thought of the possibility of failing—only of the fame and glory I was going to get when I won. I could see it. I could almost feel it. When I proclaimed that I was the "Greatest of All Time," I believed in myself. And still do.

Throughout my entire boxing career, my belief in my abilities triumphed over the skill of an opponent. My will was stronger than their skills. What I didn't know was that my will would be tested even more when I retired.

In 1984, I was conclusively diagnosed with Parkinson's disease. Since that diagnosis, my symptoms have increased and my ability to speak in audible tones has diminished. If there was anything that would strike at the core of my confidence in myself, it would be this insidious disease. But my confidence and will to continue to live life as I choose won't be compromised.

Early in 1996, I was asked to light the cauldron at the Summer Olympic Games in Atlanta, Georgia. Of course my immediate answer was yes. I never even thought of having Parkinson's or what physical challenges that would present for me.

When the moment came for me to walk out on the 140-foot high scaffolding and take the torch from Janet Evans, I realized I had the eyes of the world on me. I also realized that as I held the Olympic torch high above my head, my tremors had taken over. Just at that moment, I heard a rumble in the stadium that became a pounding roar and then turned into deafening applause. I was reminded of my 1960 Olympic experience in Rome, when I won the gold medal. Those thirty-six years between Rome and Atlanta flashed before me, and I realized that I had come full circle.

Nothing in life has defeated me. I am still "The Greatest." This I believe.

MUHAMMAD ALI *won the world heavyweight boxing championship three times. He retired in 1981 and became active in humanitarian causes, including goodwill missions to Afghanistan, North Korea, and Cuba. Ali married childhood friend Lonnie Williams in 1986.*

# The Invitation to Name Our Beliefs

~~~~~~~~

## BETH BOEHM

MY FATHER WAS A SALESMAN, BUT HE SHOULD HAVE BEEN A teacher. From the time I could read, I could not walk within arm's length of the leather wing chair in his corner of the living room without being handed a news clipping, an article, or a book off his cluttered table, and being invited to sit down on his ottoman, read the section he'd pointed to, and offer an opinion on it. But simply offering an opinion did not get me off the hook: I had to think about how holding that particular opinion would play out in other situations. I still remember a difficult conversation (it felt more like an inquisition) from the late 1970s. After my father asked me, a developing feminist, whether I was "in favor" of abortion,

I responded with a quick answer that I thought he, a devout Catholic, wanted to hear. He knew I was trying to get out the door, but he insisted on asking a series of questions aimed at getting at what I really believed: Are you against abortion in all instances? What if the mother's life is in danger? What if she had been raped? Are you against it only for yourself, or do you believe it wrong for everyone? What about those who don't have the support you have, those who are abandoned by the father, penniless and without loving parents? His questions made me look beyond him— and beyond myself—to consider those who held different beliefs.

He had a way of making every issue, even those far less controversial than abortion, complicated and of asking questions that would prevent simplistic declarations of belief. Dad knew that the world was becoming increasingly complicated and that his children would face ethical dilemmas that he had never had to, and he wanted us to be armed with values that would guide both our own actions and our attitudes toward others. He wanted us to have the courage of our convictions—the strength both to name our beliefs and to act upon them—which he thought we would have only if we had come to them through serious thought and deliberation.

My father not only expected his children to develop and express their beliefs, but he set an example by expressing his own in letters to his elected officials and to the editor of our local paper. Indeed, we joked that Dad's frequent letter writing initiated the *Dayton Daily News'* "one-letter-per-person-per-month" rule. Once, when I was an undergraduate in Washington, DC, I introduced myself to my congressman, who happened to be waiting at the same bus stop. He turned pale when he heard my last name and asked if I was related to the letter writer on Collingwood Avenue!

Conversations with my father were not always comfortable, and occasionally my brothers and I sneaked out the kitchen door to avoid passing his chair. But being raised to believe that naming my beliefs was my civic and moral duty more often than not helped me avoid acting in a way that would violate my own convictions. When my children were young, I told them to "use" me as an excuse anytime they wanted to avoid doing something that made them uncomfortable. "Simply tell your friends 'My mom won't let me do that,'" I would say. But I knew that as they got older, they would have to say "my beliefs won't let me do that," and I believe they will only be able to do that if the adults in their lives invite them to name those beliefs.

DR. BETH BOEHM *has been a professor of English at the University of Louisville for over twenty-five years, and she now serves as the dean of the School of Interdisciplinary Studies and the vice provost for Graduate Affairs. She is a wife and mother of two teenagers, both of whom are highly capable of stating their beliefs!*

# War Is Never the Answer

~⌒

## Jean Edwards

In reviewing the guidelines offered for writing a This I Believe essay, my thoughts focused on one sentence in particular: "Consider moments when belief was formed or tested or changed." For me, a radical change began to take place when I entered college in 1939. What I believed was shaken to its roots.

Prior to that time, life had seemed rather simple. Church activities, especially youth work, consumed a great deal of my time. During the summers, church camp was very important. My church congregation and my pastor were very warm and caring, providing me with a real sense of security. Our family attended services regularly. The American flag was proudly displayed in the church sanctuary alongside the Christian flag.

During 1939, Hitler began his rampage through Europe, and Great Britain joined forces to stop him. A patriotic fervor pervaded my family life in Nashville, Tennessee, where I grew up. My older brother was considering joining the Navy. Students in my church group were being drafted. We joined our neighbors in responding to the Red Cross call to roll bandages for the soldiers. And the discussion around the table centered on whether the United States should enter the war in Europe.

This was also the topic of conversation in my history class during my first year of college. The students had grown up with the conviction that there would never be another world war. Our parents had convinced us of this. We asked the teacher how it could have happened that we were considering going to war. She summed it up in one sentence, which had a profound effect upon me, "We will continue to have wars until the young men refuse to go." She was a Quaker. From experiencing that class, a new way of thinking for me began to take shape.

A similar discussion was making the rounds in our church congregation. This came to a head one Sunday morning when the pastor expressed his opinion during the sermon. He was completely opposed to entering the war. Headlines in the newspaper the next morning were two inches high: "Presbyterian Pastor Preaches Pacifism." A bitter dispute consumed our congregation. It was shocking to hear such mean words coming from church members who had loved and nurtured me. I wondered if they really believed the Sermon on the Mount. Finally the pastor left and started a new church on the outskirts of town, and about 300 members went with him.

This account of my experiences in 1939 tells only the beginning of my journey through various wars that have affected me more or less directly, including World War II, the Korean War, the Vietnam War, the Contra War in Nicaragua, the Persian Gulf War, and the wars in Iraq and Afghanistan. Looking back over these years, this is what I now believe: war is never the answer. And preparation for war is never the answer. Albert Einstein once said, "You cannot simultaneously prepare and prevent war." Yet our nation continues to live by war and weapons; it is our business, our livelihood. But in the words of the prophet Micah, "God has told you what is good; and what does the Lord require of you but to do justice, and to love kindness, and to walk humbly with your God." I believe this as much today as I did back in 1939.

JEAN EDWARDS *grew up in Nashville, Tennessee, and moved to Louisville, Kentucky, with her husband, George, after their marriage in 1947. Residents of the city from then on, the Edwardses worked together to organize a chapter of the Fellowship of Reconciliation in Louisville in 1975, establishing its office and headquarters in their own home. Mrs. Edwards has been proud to dedicate herself to this vocation ever since.*

# The Courage to Change the Things I Can

~

## Harry S. McAlpin,
### as featured in the 1950s series

BASIC IN MY LIFE HAVE BEEN THESE BELIEFS: THAT THERE ARE some things for which I am not responsible, some I cannot change, and some I can. Around recognition and acceptance of these facts, I have tried to build a philosophy by which to live in our complex society.

Forty-six years ago I was born a Negro in America. For this, of course, I was not responsible, though I am proud of it. I have traveled around the world and have learned from experience that I would rather be an American, with an inalienable right to fight against discriminations and prejudices and injustices, than to be any other nationality with a pseudo-equality—in slavery to the state, unable or afraid to express or even think my dislikes or disagreements—as is the case in Russia and other communist-controlled countries.

I had a father who regrettably died when I was fifteen years old and a senior in high school. He was a man of great principle. He abhorred injustice. He believed, in spite of the handicaps he suffered because of his color, that all men were created equal in the sight of God, and that included him and me. He instilled me with his beliefs. To live by these beliefs, I have found it necessary to develop patience, to build courage, to pray for wisdom. But despite my fervent prayers, I find it is not always easy to live up to my creed.

The complexities of modern-day living—particularly as I must face them day to day as a Negro in America—often put my creed to test. It takes a great deal of patience to accept the customs of some sections and communities, to try to fit into the crossword puzzle of living the illogic of a practice that will permit me to ride on the public buses without segregation and seating, but deny me the right to rent a private room to myself in a hotel; or the illogic of a practice which will accept me as a chauffeur for the rich who can afford it, but deny me the opportunity of driving one of the public buses I may ride indiscriminately; or the illogic of a practice which will accept me and require me to fight on the same battlefield but deny me the right to ride in the same coach on a train.

It takes a great deal of courage to put principles of right and justice ahead of economic welfare and well-being, to stand up and challenge established and accepted practices, which amount to arbitrary exercise of power by petty politicians in office or by the police. Trying to live up to my beliefs often has subjected me to both praise and criticism. How wise I have been in my choices may be known only to God. I firmly believe, however, that as an American, as a man, and as a Christian, I have been strengthened, and life about me has been made better, by the steel hardening fires through which my creed and my faith have carried me.

I shall continue to pray, therefore, a prayer I learned in the distant past, which I now count as my own: "God, give me serenity to accept the things I cannot change, courage to change the things I can, and wisdom to know the difference."

HARRY S. McALPIN *was the first African-American reporter credentialed to the White House, where he covered Presidents Roosevelt and Truman for fifty-one black newspapers. He was also a Navy war correspondent and spokesman for the Department of Agriculture. Later McAlpin practiced law in Louisville, Kentucky, and was president of the local chapter of the NAACP. He died in 1985.*

# In God Alone

~

## JOE REAGAN

IN THE FALL OF 1993, I WAS WRAPPING UP A FAILED BUSINESS venture. I was also hospitalized that year, which further wreaked havoc on my business and left us digging out from medical bills. My wife Julie and I had started a family; we had two small children—John, age two, and Sarah, age one—and Amanda on the way.

By this time in my life, I had surrendered most of my life to God. But I lived by a pious motto attributed to St. Augustine: "Pray as though everything depends on God. Work as though everything depends on you." That seemed to me like a logical division of labor. So I worked with all the self-will I could muster while praying for God's will to be done, especially to help me take care of this growing and beautiful family.

But this belief was soon to be shaken when I realized one night that fall that we had absolutely, completely run out of money. We had $25 in the checking account, no credit, and little food in the house. Some cash might be coming in about two weeks, but none until then. For someone whose self-image was completely wrapped up in winning in business and taking care of my family at home, this was devastating. Despite my hard work and tenacity, I could not change what was happening.

And then, on top of being pregnant, Julie became very painfully ill.

Julie had a friend in our parish who found out she was sick. It was not uncommon for friends to organize meals when a baby is born, but this friend had had the experience of being pregnant and sick and realized what a burden that is, and that a time such as that is when the meals would really be needed. So she sprang into action and organized ten days of meals for our family.

Now she did not know anything about our financial situation; she was just acting out her faith. But here she was at our doorstep with meals for the next day and promises of meals for the next ten days. Each evening the doorbell would ring and I would open it up to see the face of God standing there with a casserole. Those wonderful women had no idea what they were really bringing into our home and what lesson they were teaching me.

On the tenth day, Julie realized we had no milk, which was a necessity in a home with two small children. She was going to scrounge around in coat pockets in hopes of finding some milk money when the doorbell rang. There was another of Julie's friends, with a sack full of meals and two gallons of milk. Julie was absolutely shocked. "Why would you bring us milk?" she asked.

"I didn't even think about it," her friend replied, "Why wouldn't I? You have to have some milk with your meal." Again, this friend was oblivious to the true challenge we had. All my effort—my working like it was all up to me—could not even produce a gallon of milk for my family. But through these faithful, loving women, God was doing for me what I could not do for myself.

I abandoned the belief of praying like it's all up to God and working like it's all up to me, and instead I began to accept that all of my life—prayer *and* work—rests in God alone.

Not that I stopped working. But I now believe that I work by the grace of God and try most days to dedicate my work for the glory of God. What is up to me is to be still and know that God is God, and I am not.

JOE REAGAN has roots in Kentucky as a direct descendent of Daniel Boone's brother Samuel and his wife, Sarah. Mr. Reagan worked at Greater Louisville Inc., the Metro Chamber of Commerce, for fourteen years, including serving as the Chamber's CEO. Following in the footsteps of his ancestral uncle Daniel, he now lives in Missouri and serves as president and CEO of the St. Louis Regional Chamber. He and Julie are blessed with seven wonderful children.

# Courageous Surrender

~

## MARY JO KRUER

As a Hospice chaplain, I see life differently because facing death every day has given me the opportunity to gain new perspectives. When someone dies after having had an extended illness wrought with treatments, conventional or unconventional, people endearingly will say, "She sure gave it a good fight." I am beginning to question the real worth of the "good fight." What is the person fighting? Death? Why is it good to fight against all odds the act of dying? Are only fighters considered courageous?

I believe embracing death is an extremely valiant life path. Embracing, rather than resisting, takes great courage. Accepting life as it comes, welcoming each moment, lays the foundation for a peaceful existence. Accepting death as it beckons can also be filled with much peace.

The dying process is filled with constant acts of "letting go." One lets go of all that was physically near and dear, all that sustained, all that had given comfort. However, letting all these things go does not mean that one is left with "nothing." All that was is transformed. All that was binding is transformed into freedom.

I believe it is a noble act to face one's death or that of a loved one with open arms. Some cultures have already attained this marker. Our American culture, however, is well grounded in the resistance. I see people clamoring for more drugs, more treatments, more avenues of hope against the cursed outcome. I'm not discounting the medical or even religious communities for their efforts. But a more helpful approach, I believe, would be to create a simple understanding of death as a natural part of life. This is not such a simple task in our culture since death is viewed as one of the most dreaded of all experiences.

Yet, I have seen no greater peace than when someone dies. I remember the daughter who feared having her mother die in her home. Like many, she thought those memories would haunt her. Just the opposite happened. After spending time with the daughter, encouraging her to voice her concerns with me, sharing the benefits of embracing her mother's death, her fears vanished, freeing her to experience her mother's peaceful death at home. This woman now looks on her mother's death as one of the most spiritual moments she has ever experienced. Why would anyone want to resist that?

I believe it is because most people don't know that this is even an option. Just like when I was pregnant with my first child, I had heard all the horror stories of how painful it would be, and so I was naturally quite anxious. However, the Lamaze classes helped me anticipate birthing in a totally new way. I accepted it and embraced it, rather than fearing it. Education and resources made all the difference.

I believe death can be anticipated in the same way as birth in taking us to a new existence. The child in the womb has no idea what lies ahead. The child only knows contractions and movement, gasping for air and a bright light eliminating the darkness. I believe the dying experience can be transformed through a new way of viewing it, and we can all be transformed by embracing our inevitable deaths. Through the act of surrendering to the natural progression of life, death can become our final passage to freedom.

MARY JO KRUER *was born and raised in Fairfield, Kentucky, a small town in northeastern Nelson County. She now resides with her husband, Tom, on a small farm in the Botland area. She is currently the chaplain and bereavement coordinator for Hospice of Nelson County.*

# A Part of All

~⁀~

## George Ella Lyon

Several years ago I visited an Illinois Indian mound museum with my family. We entered on the ground floor and worked our way up to the third, ending on a deck that overlooks the mounds themselves, now part of a subdivision.

On the deck rail was a bronze map to help identify what we were seeing. It also offered these words: *Imagine you are a person totally dependent on the natural world for your survival.*

It was late afternoon by the time we reached that rail through a curtain of chilly spring rain. But I got white hot as I read those words. I knew they meant for us to take ourselves back in time, undo all our progress and convenience, and think *primitive.* Leaving aside the ignorance of that word applied to the rich culture of Native Americans, behind the bronze words stood a lethal lie: unlike those who came before us, we are *not* dependent on the natural world for our survival. We have air conditioning, computers, microwaves, and supermarkets. We are free of all that.

Until the power goes out.

Until the ice storm, the super storm, the earthquake. Until we can't flush the toilet.

It is the belief implied by that sentence—who wrote it? how much were they paid?—that allows us to blow up mountains to get coal, spew oil into the oceans, raise animals for slaughter in cruelty and filth. If we aren't dependent, if we are *free* from all that, what does it matter? Shouldn't we get as much as we can, as fast as we can, for as long as we can? What does it have to do with us?

What does water have to do with fish?

We are a small part of the natural world, not lords outside it. Even as our impact on creation has grown out of all proportion, that fact has not changed. It can't. With rare exceptions, we can survive less than a week without water, about two weeks without food. We still require shelter. We will still die of infection if we can't keep our skin, food, and water clean. We are finite. As individuals, we live or die in relation to the health of our food, air, and water. As a species, we live or die with the planet.

I believe in going to nature's school. When we walk through the woods, float on a lake, or wade in the surf, we have a chance to come into conscious relationship with the web of which we are a part. We can step out of our walls of abstraction into our bodies, vulnerable as any creature.

To feel small among leaves and rocks, birds and bugs, to feel infinitesimal on the edge of waves that have been breaking forever: these experiences invite us to remember our relationship with the earth which bore and sustains us. To come home.

---

GEORGE ELLA LYON's *most recent poetry collection is* Many-Storied House. *Her honors include an Al Smith Fellowship, numerous grants from The Kentucky Foundation for Women, and a Pushcart Prize nomination. A native of Harlan, Kentucky, Lyon works as a freelance writer and teacher based in Lexington.*

# Man Can Become Better

⁓

## EDMOND R. SCHLESINGER,
### AS FEATURED IN THE 1950S SERIES

THIRTY YEARS AGO, I WAS THIRTY THEN, I THOUGHT I KNEW quite well what I believe. I lived in Vienna at this time. The city was recovering from the first World War. Material and spiritual reconstruction went hand in hand. I assisted and I enjoyed.

I was brought up by my father in the belief in the inevitable progress of mankind. Yes, in 1922, the future of humanity seemed bright to me. When clouds appeared, I told myself: fulfillment takes a long time. I shall not enter the promised land—people cherishing the same ideas as I: religion. Alas, many hopes have been shattered since. The birds of visionary dreams did not arrive. Precious goods were destroyed. But the hard times had a healthy result. I began to sift the chaff from the grain. I'm still at it, still an apprentice. My cocksureness decreased. The period of orientation had its pains and its elations.

Where do I stand today? I believe in kindness as a common denominator of all human beings. They may acquire only minute traces of this kindness, hidden deep under rocks of bitterness, disappointment, discouragement. But this kindness exists in everyone. I have lived in many countries. I have lived on two continents. I'm addicted to people. I indulge myself in seeing them, in speaking to them, in knowing them. Since I can remember, I've been eager to mix with people. My various professions have enabled me to contact them out of the most different aspects. In view of my experiences, I believe man is the same everywhere, and there are neither perfect nor hopeless cases.

I don't believe we are living in the best of all possible worlds. Nevertheless, I'm compelled to believe in this world, because I live in it. I'm compelled to believe in others, because to believe in myself alone is not enough. I may hope to improve when I am able to see improvement in my fellow man. Feeling for one's fellow man is a privilege, as well as a responsibility. In Germany at the very end of the first World War, Leonard Frank wrote a book, *Man Is Good*. I've gradually softened this statement to: man can become better. Again and again I've encountered their objection. Don't you see? Does history not teach you that this earth is a wasteland and man develops only to devastate it more thoroughly? No.

A scientist at Cornell once said to me, "The more we know, the less we understand. How does research help mankind?" I answered, "In as much as research clarifies, it diminishes fear."

Since the era of the caveman, man's fear has diminished only in a tiny degree. But proportionately, man has become better. And I believe that humanity stands just at its threshold, and will wander the long, winding, arduous road toward light.

---

*Although he was born in Paris and raised in Vienna,* Dr. EDMOND R. SCHLESINGER *declared later in life: "I am a gentleman from Kentucky with a foreign accent." Schlesinger became the editor and translator for the French National Broadcasting System, earning a spot on Adolf Hitler's "Most-Wanted Political Saboteur" registry. To escape the Nazis, Schlesinger and his family immigrated to the United States in 1940, eventually settling in Louisville in 1946. Schlesinger was a longtime professor of modern languages and humanities at the University of Louisville. He died in 1968.*

# Important Strangers

~

### Leslie Guttman

THE BOOKSTORE WAS WARM AND COZY. IT WAS PACKED, maybe because people didn't realize the rain had stopped. I was on a lunch break. I got a weird feeling. Someone was looking at me.

I looked up. A woman with long, black hair about five feet away quickly looked back down at the book she was leafing through. I looked down, too. More people came in the door. The gust of air that followed them smelled clean, as if it had been freshly laundered.

I glanced up again at the dark-haired woman in time to see her slip a book into her satchel and walk off. I hesitated and then walked after her.

"Pssst," I said, pointing at the satchel. Up close, I saw that she was about thirty and probably homeless. Her khaki parka was filthy, her hair matted. The satchel was bursting with her belongings. She gave me a sorrowful look. Then she handed me the book and ran off.

The manager came up, having seen what had happened. The book was a journal designed for someone who was grieving. Someone like me. It was beautifully bound, the paper creamy and heavy. It had space to write the answers to statements like: "I miss the way you . . ." and "It's hard for me to be without you when I . . ."

"She's been wanting that book," said the manager. "She comes in all the time and looks at it. Sometimes, she puts it on hold, but then she never gets it."

Dammit! I thought. Why did I have to be such a Goody Twoshoes? When will I learn to mind my own business? Why didn't I just let her steal it?

I ran out of the store. It was raining again. I caught up with her a block away. "Did you just lose someone?" I said.

"My grandmother," she said. "I used to talk to her every day, and I miss her so much I can't stand it." I told her about my stepdad, who had just passed away. His kindness had helped knit our family together for eighteen years.

I told her to wait a second. I knew I was now in a Buddhist fable in which nothing is an accident. When I came back and handed her the book, we both stood on the curb and wept.

For the first time since my stepdad died, I felt understood—as only a stranger can understand you, without inadequacy or regret. Up until then, I had felt alone in my grief. I was reluctant to turn to my family because they were grieving, too. The love of friends had not been able to dilute my sorrow.

But because the grieving thief and I didn't know each other, I had no expectations of whether I would be understood in my grief and no fear of being disappointed if I wasn't. Since we wouldn't see each other again, I could be emotional without being embarrassed or scared it would drive someone away.

I believe life, or God, or whatever you want to call it, puts people in our path so that they can help us, or we them—or both. This encounter made me want to stay open to the chance meeting with an important stranger, to the possibility of unplanned symmetry that is luminous and magical.

LESLIE GUTTMAN *is an independent journalist who lives in Lexington, Kentucky, where she grew up. She worked at the* San Francisco Chronicle *for over a decade, and is the author of* Equine ER, *which chronicles a year inside one of the country's top hospitals for horses.*

# The Knowing

SILAS HOUSE

I BELIEVE THAT IF MORE PEOPLE WERE LIKE DOGS, WE'D ALL be a whole lot happier.

My dogs make me a better person just by being themselves. They don't care about what color I am, or whom I love, or my religion, or any of the other ridiculous things that separate us as people. They only care that I am kind to them and others. That's what should matter.

My dogs also know that giving and receiving affection are the most important things in life. Yes, eating is right up there, too. But I believe that if my dogs had to choose between lying still in a patch of sunshine while I sat beside them on the grass giving their bellies a good rub or devouring a meal of the same dog food they get every single day of their lives . . . well, I truly believe they'd choose the loving, despite their genuine devotion to gobbling down their kibble as if they might never have another morsel of food offered to them in their whole lives.

When they offer themselves up to receive adulation, they cause me to become still, to remember that most things actually can wait a few more minutes to get done because this moment right here, this moment of sitting beneath the trees with their swaying limbs, the sun warm on my face, the scent of the creek down in the woods, the birdcall in the deepest parts of those woods, and the holy world (all of it holy, every single bit of it) shimmering all about me, this moment is what life is about.

Having a dog—or any pet—makes us better people. They force us to slow down (each time I return home I have to spend a few minutes patting the belly of our outside dog, Rufus, because he'll lie down on the driveway on his back, right in my way as I'm rushing to the door; I can't refuse that and I often fold myself down onto the ground with grocery bags standing all around us to give him some loving), to pay more attention, to be kinder (especially to Pepper, who came from an abusive household before ours, and carries all of that grief in his eyes, in his damaged back, in his wariness), to give and receive affection, to be patient (especially on days when Holly Marie just doesn't really feel like going to the bathroom anytime quick), to love and love and love.

Writers aren't supposed to throw that word around much. We're supposed to be stingy with putting that on the page. But it is necessary when talking about dogs because that's what they embody. They remind us, time and time again, of the most important thing. Such a shame that we actually forget that. But we do.

I know that some people think it's a sin to think an animal has a soul, but I do. I don't care what anyone says or thinks. Because if anything in this world is close to God, it's a dog. I believe a great amount of being in touch with God is required to hear the thunder from way off, or to feel the trembling of a train miles away, or to know when someone they care about needs them, and offer comfort no matter what, and not have one tiny bit of judgment in their whole beings. I believe a sort of holiness is required to remind us that everything in this world deserves affection. Dogs know these things. They know and know and know.

Dogs make us better people. That's what I believe.

SILAS HOUSE *is the nationally bestselling author of five novels, three plays, and one work of creative nonfiction. He has been published in the* New York Times, Narrative, Newsday, Oxford American, *and many other publications. The NEH Chair of Appalachian Studies at Berea College, he also serves on the fiction faculty of the MFA in creative writing at Spalding University.*

# Definitions

~

## Sofie Tapia

I remember it clearly. I was sitting on my mom's bed staring intently at my forearm. My skin is the color of coffee mixed with cream. "Mom, look at how pretty my skin is," I said, shoving my arm in her face. She glanced up and replied, "Yes, it is." I looked at her for a moment and said bluntly, "You are no color at all." This was a simple observation made by six-year-old me, and I was only then beginning to understand how people were defined by differences in their appearance.

Growing up around predominately white people, my friends would caress my head with fascination. They would comment on my hair's cottonball-like texture and its tendency to stick straight up like a Chia Pet. My hair has always been a distinguishing characteristic, one that always made me stand out in a crowd. But this difference in my appearance never bothered me. It was normal, just something I had grown up with. I never thought of myself as different, or out of place. After all, it was only hair.

Then, something happened in middle school that brought me to racial consciousness. A group of my friends and I were sitting around the table at lunchtime, enthralled by a joke that a boy was telling. The punch line was a racist comment against African-American people. Naturally, I was offended. The boy who told the joke saw the expression on my face and stumbled over his words in trying to offer an apology. And then, trying to make me feel better, he said "It's okay, Sofie, because you're not really black!" 'Not really black?' What did *that* mean?

That is when I learned that society had an image, an expectation, of who I was supposed to be. Apparently, I don't "talk black" or "act black" enough to fit some people's expectations. There is a mold that I am supposed to fit into, one where I talk a certain way, dress a certain way, and live a certain way. And since I do not fit this mold, I therefore should not be associated with half of my identity. I don't think that boy realized that his apology was more offensive than the joke.

Although I am still young, I have evolved in my views of

my identity and how I respond to other people's ignorance about it. When people comment on my race, I attempt to respectfully explain to them how offensive and short-sighted their views are to me. It is true I have a mixed background—my mother is a white American and my dad is a black African. I embrace my heritage, but I will not allow myself to be put in a box of society's expectations for me. I believe in creating my own expectations for myself and will never let my race alone define me.

SOFIE TAPIA *grew up in Lexington, Kentucky, and is currently a sophomore at George Mason University. She is majoring in communications with a minor in global affairs.*

# Creative Solutions to Life's Challenges

~

## Frank X Walker

I BELIEVE THAT WHAT WE OFTEN CALL SURVIVAL SKILLS IS simply creativity at work.

When I think about how my mother fed all seven of us, making us think that every day was a "different meal," I still appreciate how much a creative cook can do with a single potato.

And it wasn't just in the kitchen. She would flip her old Singer sewing machine upright, study pictures in books and magazines, then make ethnic versions of those same dolls and stuffed animals to sell at church fundraisers. Without a TV in the house to distract us, we made the dolls come to life, filling the hollow fabric sleeves one fistful of cotton at a time.

My mother made her own clothes and all my sisters' prom and wedding dresses. I always knew when she was making something, because she would be singing or humming. She sang all the way through her home correspondence courses in floral design and interior decorating. She made being creative as normal as breathing and encouraged our participation by telling us that "idle hands and minds were the devil's workshop."

I believe that happy children are those given the freedom to be expressive, to discover, to create their own "refrigerator-door" masterpieces. I remember mixing tempera paints with powdered detergent and painting the Baskin-Robbins windows every Christmas season. Not for money, but for all the ice cream I could eat. And every time I saw people look up at the window and smile, I knew I was getting the best part of the deal.

I believe that the highest quality of life is full of art and creative expression and that all people deserve it. I believe in a broad definition of what art is and who artists are: barbers, cooks, auto detailers, janitors, and gardeners have as much right to claims of artistry as designers, architects, painters, and sculptors. Every day, our streets and school buses become art galleries in the form of perfectly spiked hair, zigzagging cornrows, and dizzying shoelace artistry.

My first collection of art was a milk crate full of comic books. I survived the projects and my teenage years inspired by my favorite character, the Black Panther, who had only his mind and no superpowers, and Luke Cage, the thick-skinned, inner-city Hero for Hire. By the time my "bookish" reputation and thick glasses became a target for the neighborhood bullies, I responded by composing juvenile but truly "heroic" rhyming couplets in my head.

Ever since high school, words have continued to serve as my first weapon of choice and my salvation. Many of life's challenges need creative solutions. I believe creativity—in all its many forms—can change the way we think and operate. Celebrating the creativity around us helps maintain our sanity and keeps us happy.

FRANK X WALKER *is assistant professor of English at Eastern Kentucky University. He coined the word "Affrilachian" to describe African-Americans living in Appalachia, and he helped found a group of Affrilachian poets. Walker is the author of three collections of poetry and was awarded a prestigious Lannan Literary Fellowship in 2005. He was appointed to serve as Kentucky Poet Laureate for 2013–2014.*

# *Ability*

~

## Becki Turner

As a senior in high school, I volunteered to help out during the North Laurel Special Olympics. Of course, it was more of a chore than an honor to me then. I volunteered in order to get out of my classes for the day.

Students with mental and physical disabilities filled the football field. Volunteer students and teachers were in charge of the different stations where the athletes would perform such feats as running, jumping, throwing balls, and most important, having fun. Other volunteers, such as me, were assigned to work with the athletes, guiding them from station to station, keeping them safe, and making sure they were actually having fun.

Brian was my guy. With a mild mental disability that also affected his physical agility, Brian was jerky, at best, when he tried to run. His aim may have been right on when he lined up to throw a ball, but his erratic movements stopped him from making the shot. I wondered how he would ever enjoy such a day. I thought that the students from special education would surely see the day as patronizing and insulting, especially since there were nondisabled students thrown in the mix who would see their shortcomings. I thought this was a severe waste of my time.

But was I ever wrong! Never had I seen such determination and such fun. Brian, and all the other athletes, could not have been more excited if it had been Christmas morning. Brian rushed from station to station. He could barely speak for laughing and jumping with excitement. He was happy just to be included.

Nearly a full year later, I ran into Brian at a church my husband and I were visiting. By then, I had graduated from high school, and Brian was in tenth grade. Brian was sitting on the second seat from the back when I walked into the church. He immediately recognized me and stood up. Pushing people out of his way, he hurried over to me, threw his arms around me, and kissed my cheek.

"Do you remember me? Do you remember that day at school?" He recalled details I had forgotten. He remembered medals and ribbons that he earned. And then he said something that has stayed with me since that day: "I did it, Becki; I did it."

That day at the Special Olympics, Brian knew that he was "abled," not disabled. And that day at church is when I came to believe that everyone has abilities, including me. I just have to focus on the things I can do, not the things I can't. Maybe I cannot play basketball, but I can keep score. Maybe I cannot win a marathon, but I can finish one. Maybe I cannot be Stephen King, but I can tell my own story. I believe in focusing on abilities.

BECKI TURNER *is a recent graduate of Midway College with a degree in elementary education with a certification in special education. She is also a volunteer firefighter with Campground Volunteer Fire Department in London, Kentucky. She has a passion for community service and helping others advocate for themselves. In her free time, she enjoys reading and spending time with her husband, Chris, and her two children, Jacob and Gracie.*

# Our Brother's Keepers

&#8667;

## Stephen Mershon

Working during my college years solidified the belief system that was ingrained in me as a child. To me, it seems that our beliefs evolve from fate, from the way we play the cards that we were dealt at birth, and from our childhood roots and wings that prepare us for and carry us into adult life. My fate was to have been born with an emotional silver spoon in my mouth and to have been raised in the middle of a large, loving Catholic family. I had wonderful experiences as an altar boy and even considered the seminary. But then I met the woman who has been my wife for thirty-seven years, and the Catholic seminary was no longer an attractive option.

During college, I worked for several years as a Teamster truck driver and for several years at Our Lady of Peace, a psychiatric hospital. Interacting with people at both jobs taught me that I could never make a quick judgment about someone, that I never completely had the whole picture within my grasp.

Particularly, a hospital patient was not just a patient. He was a reflection of his genetic makeup and of his family and upbringing. He was his past, his present, and his future—his hopes and dreams, his loves and disappointments, his unreconciled problems and unanswered questions, and his knowledge of what (if anything) he had to go home to.

I learned patience and tolerance. I learned to move slowly, to ask a lot of questions, and to be open to unexpected possibilities. And I learned how critically important it is to listen, especially to those with whom we disagree.

I learned that the truth is difficult to discern, that one's eyes are the entrance to one's soul, and that looking into another's eyes is like looking into a mirror and seeing the common humanity that we all share, seeing that combination of saint and sinner that we all are.

I believe in the Yogic blessing of Namaste, that the spark of divinity in me recognizes the divine in you. Perhaps the best summation of my beliefs is the old saying: "There, but for the grace of God, go I."

I believe that there is a grace—call it God or Fate, the

Tao, Mother Nature, or whatever that power is that deals the cards at birth—and that that grace, which is beyond comprehension, unites us all. But for that grace, any of our circumstances could be drastically different.

So on a fundamental, universal level, I believe that we are all connected and that we are all truly our brother's keepers. This I believe.

STEPHEN MERSHON *was a circuit court judge in Jefferson County, Kentucky, where he heard cases ranging from death penalty trials to Brown & Williamson v. Jeffrey Wigand. Mershon was voted judge of the year in 2007 by the Louisville Bar Association.*

# Dancing to the Music

∽

## AMANDA JOSEPH-ANDERSON

A MULTITUDE OF ORNATE SQUARES DECORATED A HUNTER-green carpeted floor. The Beatles and a few other notable artists were strung out in no particular order. I studied the album art, fascinated by the pictures and stories they told. I can recall creating my own dialogue for *Sgt. Pepper's Lonely Hearts Club Band* to better understand the meaning and purpose behind such flamboyant attire. What a necessary mess my mother and I had made.

This cyclical game we had played many times before. We would pull out all of my mother's old vinyl and designate a playlist. I picked mostly by the album's pictures, my mother by an artist's credibility and sound. I was a young child at the time; I didn't understand the dynamics of music.

The excitement and anticipation would build as the automatic arm positioned itself above a disk of splendor. The silver Pioneer would belt out sounds from the heavens. We then interlocked hands and twirled. Life would be forgotten in this world of ours. Our feet didn't stop until we paid homage to each tune. At no other time in my life can I remember such bliss and happiness.

I would always catch my mother turning the music up louder when she wanted to sing, in order to drown out her own voice. Nevertheless, I heard it, and it was beautiful.

She created beauty with such ease, just like those moments.

We would fade into our world for several hours. We ignored all the outside distractions. Our philosophy encouraged others to join us, or leave us alone. We were usually left alone. We danced like tribesmen waiting for the rain.

It took me years to realize the ulterior motives behind our musical endeavors. Of course my mother was very interactive with me when I was young. I have many fond memories of studying, playing games, and talking about fantasy worlds of dragons and fairies with her. But listening to music seemed to be her choice of play.

When we listened to music, I caught my mother in pure nostalgia. As we danced she would share fond moments of her life. It would almost bring her to tears. Reminiscing was always difficult for her because she had come from a happier place.

We always struggled as a family. My father was a verbally abusive alcoholic who favored breaking our spirits every time he drank. This was the "outside world" and the "distractions" that we would drown out with music.

My mother tried to instill in me the same happiness that she had been so accustomed to in her earlier years. She protected me and found a means of escape from the ugliness of our reality. And with the sounds of her music, she preserved my psychological well-being as well.

I realize now that our hours playing records and dancing together were more than just playtime—they bonded us and made us stronger than ever. And in so doing, I believe my mother made our love never ending, just like the infinite circle of an old LP.

---

AMANDA JOSEPH-ANDERSON *is an elementary school teacher in Jenkins, Kentucky, where she lives with her mother, husband, and daughter. After becoming a mother herself, Ms. Joseph-Anderson feels blessed to have such a wonderful mother as a role model for raising her own little girl.*

# A Good and Useful Life

BARRY BINGHAM SR.,
AS FEATURED IN THE 1950S SERIES

I BELONG TO THE GENERATION OF AMERICANS WHO GREW UP after World War I. Many of us pulled away from religion because we could not see in it the answer to the two things we wanted most in life: freedom and happiness. Even now it's a little difficult for me to talk about the things I believe in because my generation was embarrassed by faith. We tried to live without it. Our pursuit of happiness grew more and more feverish, and we kept running faster and faster without finding our goal.

Then the War gave us a chance to stop and take bearings. I spent many months on a Pacific island where, for the first

time in years, I really had time to think. Many others have
told me of having this same experience. I found that I could
not go on running through the strange and often terrifying
forest of modern life without a light to guide me. I could
still see the spark of faith gleaming faintly in the distance. I
have been trying ever since to work my way back to it.

I believe each of us must accept his full share of responsibility in life. My generation tried to run away from
responsibility; we tried to avoid growing up. I have a feeling
that this is especially an American weakness which we all
inherit to some extent, this unwillingness to accept matu-
rity. We are a young race living in a young country. I have
found that those who are young in heart are the happiest
people in the world. But those who stay young in character,
beyond the years of growing up, are the unhappiest.

It seems to me that the code of responsibility, here, lies
in the Parable of the Talents in the New Testament. That
simple story explains that all men are not given equal endow-
ments or opportunities, and that they are not expected to
produce equal results. The parable makes clear that the man
who is given five talents, or five pieces of money, has an obligation to produce a greater sum on the Day of Reckoning
than the man who starts with only two talents or one. It is
the degree of effort and of dedication that counts.

Of course, I do not argue that a man can meet all the
problems of life merely by embracing responsibility and

full self-reliance. The strongest among us is worth nothing without faith in a force far stronger than all our strength and wisdom combined. Yet, I believe that I must try to merit God's friendship in the calm days of my life if I am to stretch out and grasp His hand at those moments when the best of human effort fails.

We Americans of my generation have wasted years in a fruitless search for happiness and freedom. A great many of us are now beginning to realize that a happy life is a good and useful one. As to the absolute independence we have sought in vain, the *Book of Common Prayer* could have told us all along that "the answer is in God, whose service is perfect freedom."

---

BARRY BINGHAM SR. *was the long-time owner, editor, and publisher of the* Courier-Journal *and the* Louisville Times. *His family's leadership of the newspapers, as well as radio and TV properties in Kentucky, led to numerous journalism awards, including multiple Pulitzer Prizes. Bingham received an honorary knighthood from England and the Legion of Honor from the French government. He died in 1988.*

# The Stillness of the Library

⁓

## Clint Morehead

I believe in studying.

I often find a room in my school's library that reminds me of a cell in a monastery. The room is white and perfectly still. Here, I move fluidly through my notes, textbook, atlas of human anatomy, and back again, without the distraction of even a breath. For me, studying has become a solitary ritual, but I am not alone. There are other students in identical rooms, heads hinged down, shoulders hovered above fiberglass tables, reading as if they were searching for something elsewhere.

This library was built forty years ago when no architect seemed to care much about aesthetics. The walls and ceilings are a mixture of stones and pieces of shells, stuck together in a sea of gray. A rusted black and yellow sign bolted near the entrance designates it as a fallout shelter. Now, inclement weather is what sounds the sirens and sends the crowds inside. I sometimes hear them from my little room, raise my head from my books, crack the door, and watch as the drenched street dwellers mill among the stacks. After a few minutes, I return and figure out where I left off.

I believe in those rooms. And in libraries. I also believe in kitchens, coffee shops, park benches, and the shade of oak trees. These places allow studying to temporarily remove me from this uncertain, sometimes tragic world. It's a kind of asylum. When I focus down into my books, the pages are all I see, and my thoughts are all I hear. Everything else disappears. Studying becomes a communion in which I read and assimilate and grow. It steadies me. It flings me back toward myself like a reflection, until I have but one focus: the insightful person I hope to be.

At the end of the day, I return to studying the way one returns home. After dinner, I drive against the flow of traffic back to the library. In my sterile room, I seat myself. It is only me, this simple student, some lecture notes, a couple books, and a pen. The laws of physics are here too, pressing me deep into this cold chair. The world is now silenced. My eyes scan what's laid before me. Here, in this human embryology text, is an illustration of the primitive structures of the human heart, the *bulbus cordis* and *conus arteriosis*. And over there is the adult heart, in full developed form. My eyes shift from one picture to the other. I take more notes, doodle, stare at a blank wall, and let my eyes adjust. Somewhere in all this, a synapse fires. A new pathway forms. So *this* is how the heart came to be shaped the way it is! But I feel something separate from that. Learning something new is like a small epiphany. I finally get it.

---

DR. CLINT MOREHEAD *was born, raised, and educated in Louisville, Kentucky, and is now a palliative medicine doctor in San Diego, California. His work has been featured in* Becoming A Doctor: From Student to Specialist, Doctor-Writers Share Their Experiences *(W. W. Norton, 2010), the* Louisville Review, *and the* Journal of Palliative Medicine. *He is a 2010 winner of the Al Smith Fellowship for creative nonfiction and founder of The Kentucky Books for Patients Project, an organization that places books by Kentucky authors in cancer centers across the state. He wrote this essay in 2005 as a first-year medical student in Louisville.*

## Demons and Dust

~⁓

### Tori Murden McClure

I have demons. So what? People who have no demons are like people who have no sense of humor. They are dull. I am highly educated. So I feel no shame in telling teenagers that I rowed a boat alone across the Atlantic Ocean because I was *stupid*. Most women do not need to row three thousand miles to figure out that love and friendship are good things. Most women just get it.

My personal demon is a sense of helplessness. I have a brother, Lamar. He is intellectually disabled. When we were young, our family moved every three or four years. New kids on any block are always tested, often teased, and sometimes hazed. Lamar and I were accustomed to all three. I always tried to protect my brother, but I was not always successful.

When I was about twelve, Lamar and I were getting to know and be known at a new playground. I was playing basketball. Lamar was standing in his usual place at the edge of the action. A boy picked up a rock and threw it at my brother. As the boy reached out to pick up a second rock, I tackled him. I disappeared into a swirl of fists and feet. Strong hands pulled me off the boy and hauled him away for questioning.

The judge and jury that afternoon was a boy named Eric Fee. Like me, Eric would have been about twelve years old. Lamar and I were accustomed to finding ourselves at the center of neighborhood controversies. They never turned out well for us. I had read about "justice," but I had never seen it in action. Then, something inexplicable happened. Eric Fee hauled the rock-throwing boy over to Lamar and made him apologize. I could hardly believe my ears. Once the apology was complete, Eric called all the children on the playground into a circle.

Eric explained that my brother could not defend himself. He declared that Lamar was to be left alone. If anyone taunted or teased Lamar, Eric promised that he would settle the score. Someone asked about me. Eric glanced in my direction and said, "I think she can take care of herself." By his actions, a twelve-year-old boy created peace and justice out of thin air, and I watched compassion finish ahead of competition. I went out and followed Eric's example, as much as I could and as often as I could.

With each passing year, I grew wiser, more competent, and more powerful, but no matter how hard I tried I could not make justice perfect. I could not make it reliable. Time after time, I found myself jousting with injustices that were too big for me to tackle. Each time the helplessness wore me down, I settled for doing something easy like climbing a tall mountain, skiing across a frozen continent, or rowing a boat alone across an ocean. Eventually, I came to understand that I could bicycle to the moon, but it would not make me any less human. We are each of us an amalgam of dust and divinity. The dust is essential. It is our brokenness, our helplessness that make us human.

I believe that love and friendship are the things that make our humanity bearable. Each of us is mortal, and, like Eric Fee, each of us is capable of being heroic. We need not accept realities that are not in tune with our hearts. We may not succeed in stealing fire from heaven, but the majesty of humanity lies in our willingness to keep trying.

TORI MURDEN MCCLURE *is the president of Spalding University. She is a graduate of Smith College, Harvard University, the University of Louisville, and Spalding University. Ms. McClure skied 750 miles across Antarctica to geographic South Pole, and she was the first woman and first American to row solo across the Atlantic Ocean. Her book is titled* A Pearl in the Storm.

# Change Decision

BECCA TAYLOR

I KNOW THAT MANY OF THE BELIEFS I HOLD SO CLOSELY today will fall by the wayside in the coming years, as I get older. Those values that I continue to hold will most likely alter themselves somehow a decade from now. I try to avoid verbalizing too many beliefs. Some beliefs, when spoken aloud in the presence of others, only make me look foolish later. Like how I used to believe that it was acceptable to drive drunk or shoplift items priced under fifty bucks. Some things just change as I learn and grow. So at the risk of looking like an idiot if my youthful ideals are overrun by the cynicism that comes from experiencing reality, I'll tell you what I believe.

I believe that I can change the world. I will feed a child, listen to a dying man's regrets, and comfort those in pain. I will have an open mind. I will vote. I will embrace diversity. I will recycle and not litter. I will give freely to charities. I will be polite. I will volunteer. I will turn the other cheek. I will love the unlovable. My consistent failure will not allow for pride, so I will laugh pleasantly when detractors mock my efforts. I will persevere knowing that one person, joined with others for a common goal, will have a mighty impact. I believe in my idealism, if only for the way it makes me feel. This belief fills me with hope.

On days that I don't believe, the future looks bleak, and depression starts to creep in. I become overwhelmed by the enormity of issues such as AIDS and homelessness. When I don't believe, I feel complacent and bored. I can spend all day watching talk shows on television. This is why I have to believe.

When I don't believe, my senses are dulled. My husband's embrace feels weak and unsure. My food tastes bland, and wine just makes me belligerently drunk. I only smell vomit and piss when I don't believe. This is why I have to believe.

When I don't believe, my ears filter out the sounds of laughter. When I don't believe, I only hear shouting and curses. I hear horns honking and tires screeching and then the crash. When I don't believe, I stop listening to music. This is why I have to believe.

When I don't believe, I see sadness and hardship everywhere I look. My mind replays scenes of documentaries showing decaying bodies piled on the street. When I don't believe, I can't read a good book. This is why I have to believe.

I truly hope that my beliefs do not leave me looking like a fool later in life. But I don't think this one will, because my belief is also a decision. I will change the world.

BECCA TAYLOR *now lives with her husband and family in a yellow house in Richmond, Virginia. She is a psychiatric nurse and tries to work as little as possible, so as to stay relatively sane. While she loves Virginia, she reminisces sometimes about her life in Louisville, where she learned to love running, especially in Waterfront Park.*

# Administering Our Gifts
## for All of Mankind

~

### GANT GAITHER,
### AS FEATURED IN THE 1950S SERIES

FOR FORTY-FIVE YEARS I HAVE BEEN AN ACTIVE SURGEON
in western Kentucky. Out of that life, daily taking into my
hands for surgical care the lives of many people of all ages
and stations, I have accumulated a store of contacts with
mankind. It is from this I derive my beliefs: that the motto,
*noblesse oblige,* given me at graduation from high school, is
paramount in service of man, to man and his Creator. I
believe that those of us favored by nature with God's gifts of
skill, supplemented by education and experience, by learn-

ing and wisdom, have a great privilege to administer these gifts for all mankind assiduously—rich or poor, black or white, starched collar or overalls, to each alike.

I inherited from a wonderful father the common touch. I love people, especially those whom we often call the "underdog," "little people," those whom life has hard bitten. I early believed that I must not willingly hurt anyone's feelings—though not to be mealy mouthed—if the issue were between right or wrong; that I should not be exalted by success nor downcast by failure; that I should be kindly in my thoughts about people and have an understanding of human weakness that would keep me from ever being harshly critical. These and many more like them became my early beliefs. They have conditioned my personal and professional life ever since.

Thus I came to believe I should, by no act of mine today, put forth any less than the best I have within me to give. I have striven, therefore, to foster this belief by study, thought, and action. In short, I believe the echoes of my past thinking, and doing, project themselves upon the sounding board of my present moment, creating visions for my life of tomorrow. This interaction of echo and vision determines what I am and do today. But this interaction must be practical for the moment, be it 1917, at the beginning of World War I when volunteer surgeons were needed in the Army Medical Corp; or again, practical for 1949, working with alcoholics and morphine addicts in each home community—its great problem of then and now. These have been some of the active challenges to my belief, above and beyond my surgery—which in itself is a jealous and bewitching mistress.

The expression "clear thinking" is important from my point of view, not allowing myself to be swept aside by the vagaries and popular foibles of the moment—that is, not too far. I have not been infallible and have had to back up at times to get myself once more on the right thinking track. It has made for me a life that I have enjoyed, filled with a terrific amount of hard work, not too many holidays, many failures and disappointments; much to rejoice over. Best of all, at 69 I still have my visions and can go forward into my 70s with my beliefs, dented at times, but still valid.

*Born in 1884, Dr. Gant Gaither practiced surgery for over half a century in his native town of Hopkinsville, Kentucky, as the town's first college-trained surgeon. Gaither attained the rank of captain in World War I, and during World War II he gave free surgical care to the families of servicemen in Campbellsville. Gaither eventually became the president of the Kentucky State Medical Association, and he served as president of the board of trustees at Hopkinsville's Jennie Stuart Hospital for fifteen years. Gaither died in 1968.*

# Learning to Parent

~~~~

MIKE DWYER

I BECAME A FATHER AT THE AGE OF NINETEEN, KNOWING IN the back of my mind that I would never raise my daughter as part of a couple with her mother. I correctly guessed that our relationship could not withstand the pressures of parenting at such a young age. I was also scared and immature, unprepared for the great responsibility that was placed on me, but I was determined to succeed.

Being the kind of person who finds comfort through the written word, I looked for answers in books and magazines. I searched online using depressing terms like "noncustodial parent" and "single father." There was good advice out there and I took much of it to heart, but I still kept searching for that one guiding principle that trumped all others. I finally found it, just a few weeks before my daughter was born. I must admit I don't remember where it came from, and I apologize to the author for not giving him or her the credit that is due. It simply read:

*"The best parents are the ones who never forget what it's like to be a kid."*

That rule has not let me down once in nineteen years as a parent. I was the first dad down the slide behind my daughter, and I will still do anything to make her laugh. I try not to embarrass her when she's with her friends, and I tried to be kind to the first boy that came to our door for a date. I also try to put myself in her shoes before I hand out punishments, which is perhaps the hardest test of my guiding principle.

I spent many years as a noncustodial parent, co-parenting as best I could with my daughter's mother. Then in 2004, I married the woman of my dreams. Her love and support allowed me to eventually gain joint custody of my daughter when she was sixteen. When we married I also gained a stepdaughter who is different from my daughter in almost every way, presenting new challenges. We have created a blended family that we are proud of and of course my parenting philosophy has evolved over time.

Like many parents, I believe that my daughters have taught me far more than I will ever teach them. In so many ways, we have grown up together. Still, I am far from perfect, and there is a regrettable gap between my beliefs and my actions. My challenge is to try to make that gap smaller and smaller with each passing year. I have many goals for myself, both professionally and personally, but at the end of the day, none of them matters if I fail as a parent. Being a parent has been one of the greatest gifts of my life, and every good parent I know has achieved their success because they realized the same thing.

*Mike Dwyer is a writer in Louisville, Kentucky. His daughter, Kelsey, whom he wrote about in his essay, is now a beautiful and intelligent nineteen-year-old who lives with him full-time. The rest of his family members are his wife, Kim, stepdaughter, Kayleigh, two dogs, and two cats.*

# A Lifetime of Story

───⌒───

## Erin Wathen

I BELIEVE IN SHARING STORIES.

I have a picture of my grandmother sitting in a lawn chair, holding me in her lap. I am holding a book larger than my three-year-old self, as she reads to me. Or maybe I am "reading" to Grandma, having memorized the events of every picture and each turn of the page. Whatever the case, the photo captures the gift of story—read and written, spoken and lived—that was her legacy.

On a November night years later, my mother and I were in the car, traveling to be with my grandmother for the last part of her story. On the way, we began to make funeral plans, which included using some of Grandma's own writing in the service. A debate ensued as to which of us had the box containing her journals, poetry, and unpublished autobiography. My mother and I began to panic, each becoming more certain the other had Grandma's papers. Both of us had moved in the past year, and we felt sure we wouldn't have thrown away something so precious, but we also knew how easily we could have misplaced the ordinary box.

Later that night, as we faced the real loss of my grandmother, the idea of having lost her story was even more devastating. Death itself is natural. But stories are to be kept and treasured, connecting generations beyond anything we can see or touch or capture in a photograph. I felt I had lost Grandma twice.

I was so relieved when my mother emerged from her basement a few hours later, holding a small, white box. I soon realized, though, that I had not really feared the loss of Grandma's story. It was to be found in many places outside that box. Growing up I simply hadn't valued it, hadn't listened closely enough. As she told stories of her childhood in rural Kentucky, recalled her family, and reflected on the changing world, my mind had wandered in typical childhood, then teen-age fashion. Even as an adult, my attention lacked the sort of reverence that a lifetime—any lifetime—of story deserves.

Now as a minister, I preach stories of wilderness and wandering, devastation and hope, renewal and transformation. My goal is to connect these biblical stories to the story of God's continued activity in the world, and to the stories of the members of our community of faith. It's extraordinary to me that people still come together to worship, to serve, and to participate in each other's life stories. I share in their journeys, too, giving thanks for the grace of God in these everyday gifts.

My grandmother was wise enough to know the value of her story. I was blessed to have shared in her life and privileged to be with her in death. The experience reminds me there's not such a great divide between sacred and secular. It's all about how we tell the story.

---

*A Kentucky native,* REV. ERIN WATHEN *serves as the senior pastor of Saint Andrew Christian Church in Olathe, Kansas. Her blog, www.irreverin.com, explores the journey of progressive faith, and the sacred revealed in everyday things. Wathen and her husband, Jeremy, have two small children.*

# Tradition and Traditional Subversion

⁓

## Cari Leigh Moore

In southeastern Kentucky, I walk out my door and into the heart and mind of God. God has blessed our land with immense biodiversity, a natural water purification system, and more miles of running water than any state besides Alaska.

My great-uncle Kell used to collect water in a gallon jug, straight from the hillside. When he came to visit, he brought a paper poke (a bag) full of bubblegum, and a plastic jug of mountain water. It remains some of the sweetest, purest water I've ever tasted. It was a gift, like the unlocked pantry of the backwoods.

When my grandmother was a child, she picked yeller

root and sang. My relatives taught me how to forage for wild food. These harvests provide food, medicine, and money. They're family bonding time, a way to pass on knowledge and connect to ancestors and the earth, a lesson in self-reliance. Sometimes we share our harvest with neighbors, building community bonds.

My grandparents, who were like parents to me, have passed away. If I have children, they'll never meet them, but I take solace in the culture and land that I love. I will take them into the untended garden of the earth, and teach them what I've been taught, so they can begin to connect with over ten generations of ancestors who did this before them.

Today, the creeks where I played, staring at my toes through clear waters, run orange. While I used to catch and release crawdads with my father, pollution has left some creeks so full of sediment, they're suffocating to death. While I drank pure water from the hillside, many of my loved ones can't drink from their own taps.

Some extol the virtues of reclaimed mountaintop removal sites, but when I walk upon them, I see nothing to sustain myself—just a handful of nonnative plants. I see no streams of life-giving water, just rock-lined ditches. I don't feel my ancestors, or God. And I don't feel at home.

Our ancestors knew how to survive without this industry, and we'll have to remember how. The US Geological Survey has said that we have decades, not centuries, of economically recoverable coal left in central Appalachia. I believe we can build a new economy on a combination of traditional jobs and new jobs based on old resources.

But I also believe we must reconnect with our communities and remember our subversive roots. Our people fought coal scrip, coal camps, and the broad form deed. They fought for the union. And they continue to fight poor working conditions, strip mining, and now mountaintop removal.

More than anything, I believe in healthy, consensual, sustainable tradition, and in alternatives to unhealthy traditions. And I believe Appalachia, if it will rise to the occasion, has both.

CARI LEIGH MOORE *is a multigenerational Appalachian and a native of southeastern Kentucky. A food service worker, CNA, and jewelry artisan, she is presently pursuing a degree in biology at Berea College. In her spare time, she is an environmental, social justice, and anti-mountaintop-removal activist. She has been published in the journal* Blood and Thunder: Musings on the Art of Medicine, *on the Kentuckians for the Commonwealth's blog, and on CoLab Radio's blog. She lives in Garner, in Knott County.*

# *Global Citizens*

～

## Elizabeth George

I believe there is more than one way to live in the world.

I have been blessed to experience life and love in several cultures. My work took me to England, where I lived for over six years. My marriage took me into an Iranian family who considers me one of their own. When I left the United States, I was excited about an adventure. When I returned here eleven years ago, I was surprised how much the experience had changed me. During my time in London, I was able to see my country from a distance and identify how growing up in America had shaped the person I had become.

My experiences with my Iranian in-laws in London presented great challenges and rewards. Iranians place a huge emphasis on family, which translates to many days spent together, often with multiple generations present. The Iranians teach the importance of respect, and their traditions reinforce this practice. In Iranian culture, everything of yours is mine and everything of mine is yours. Once, when I complimented my sister-in-law's earrings, she immediately took them off and gave them to me.

My global experiences have enriched my life in so many ways. I have a hunger for travel and the fresh perspectives it provides me. Yet, these experiences can fill me with conflicting emotions. I am overwhelmed by the selfless generosity of my in-laws even while I struggle to understand the differences in personal boundaries that I thought were the same for everyone. Reconciling these diverse expectations challenges my sense of what is normal and right. I discover that while my American family and my Iranian in-laws share the same values, we have a very different way of interpreting them.

We left England and my husband's family to raise our children in Louisville, where they could live among my extended family. It has been a truly wonderful experience. My challenge now is to ensure our children understand both their American and Iranian heritage, and grow up as people who see difference as an opportunity to learn. People raised in the United States tend to have such a strong sense of pride in what it means to be an American that it can sometimes keep us from seeing the value to be gained from embracing other perspectives.

That's one reason why my husband and I strive to raise our children as global citizens. In all our travels with them, we encourage them to be keen observers of the cultures we visit. We want our children to understand and be sensitive to the differences among people around the globe. Perhaps they'll even learn how to help bridge some of the gaps that too often divide us.

I believe every culture provides an important contribution to a world so much in need of balance and tolerance. If I am able to appreciate instead of criticize the values and beliefs of others, then I will find the right balance in my own life.

---

ELIZABETH GEORGE *is a communications director in Louisville, Kentucky. She continues to feed her curiosity about world cultures through frequent travel with her husband and two daughters.*

# God Is the Father of All Men

～

## OSCEOLA DAWSON,
### AS FEATURED IN THE 1950S SERIES

BASIC TO, AND UNDERLYING ALL MY BELIEFS, IS MY BELIEF IN God and the Bible, the only infallible guide for human conduct. Should I lose my belief in God, in Christ and the Bible, life would be meaningless, without further reason for existence.

Concurrent with my belief in the fatherhood of God is my belief in the brotherhood of man. Out of one blood, God made the nations. Either God is the father of all men, or he isn't the father of any. Either all men are brothers or none of them are related.

I see each individual not as the member of some in or out

group, but as a member of a human family—a child of God under my brother. I cannot accept the doctrine of the superiority or inferiority of racist nations or individuals. Creeds, ideas, and ideals are all useless unless translated into action. "Be what thou seemest, live thy creed. Hold up to the world the torch divine." Therefore, I have pledged myself to help my fellow countrymen reach their goal of real democracy based on the brotherhood of man, by fighting the terrible evils of segregation and discrimination based on a denial of such brotherhood.

Because God is love, I believe all actions should be prompted by the spirit of love. We should attend school for the love of learning; work for the love of work; administer to human needs because we love humanity. I believe that true greatness lies in service. "He that would be greatest among you, let him be the servant of all." The happy man is the man who gives himself wholeheartedly and unreservedly to some worthy cause. One who fails to do this has missed the joy of living.

I believe in the home as the foundation of society. World peace cannot be realized until peace is realized in that most intimate of all human relations, that of husband and wife. I believe in the education of the whole man. It is the whole man that works, not an intellect in a vacuum. Jesus grew in wisdom and stature, earning favor with God and man. I believe there is a dignity in honest toil that belongs not to the display of wealth or the luxury of fashion. The man who drives the plow, or with cunning fingers plies the tools of his craft, is as truly the servant of his country as is a soldier in battle or the statesman in the senate.

I believe that each individual must build his own life. "Take what thou hast, oh soul of mine, and build thine own house of happiness." If one builds a life with the tools he has, he can be happy. The capacity to make the best of a situation and to adjust to it is what makes for success.

Climaxing my beliefs and in keeping with my fundamental belief, I believe that God, through Christ, is the answer to the problems of the universe, and that real Christianity must stand at the foundation of every worthwhile life or nation. "Where accept the Lord build the house, they labor in vain but build it."

---

OSCEOLA DAWSON *was born in 1906 in Roaring Springs, Kentucky. After graduating from high school as valedictorian at age sixteen, Dawson started teaching at rural schools and eventually taught at the West Kentucky Vocational School for more than twenty years. Dawson was an active NAACP member, and she especially fought for equal employment opportunities for African-Americans at the federal atomic energy plant near Paducah. Many considered her the backbone of Paducah's black community. Osceola Dawson died in 1963.*

# Touching the Divine

⟆

## Jason Howard

Every few weeks, I make a pilgrimage to CD Central in Lexington, my local record store, to while away an hour or so, thumbing through rows upon rows of compact discs and vinyl. This is a time-tested journey for me, one I have taken in cities too numerous to count. I go in search of new music, which I inevitably find—the latest release from long-time favorites like Rosanne Cash or Teddy Thompson, to more recent discoveries such as Caitlin Rose and Emeli Sandé—but I also make this trip for something more.

I come to these buildings to worship, to retreat into some inner sanctuary and commune only with the music and the artists who have created it. Here, within these hallowed walls layered with posters and shelves of box sets, I turn myself over to ritual. I hear my own private Eucharist coming from the speakers scattered throughout the store. I recite a liturgy of familiar lyrics, commune with relics of timeworn vinyl. I take in the familiar incense of must and mold, paying tribute to images of singers like Nina Simone and John Lennon that have been cut from worn album covers and posted on the walls—Stations of the Cross. I make my offering at the cash register, an attempt to keep these churches and their ministers going. When this service ends and I exit back into the world, I go in peace, eager to share the good news of my finds with friends.

This ceremony has its roots in my childhood. As an only child, I spent many an afternoon in front of my father's RCA turntable in his library, kneeling on the orange shag carpet, absorbing the catholic tastes of his record collection—the sounds of Ray Charles, Johnny Cash, the Beatles, Barbra Streisand, Herb Alpert, and the Andrews Sisters. There, in that room, surrounded by vinyl and books, I slowly made a connection that endures in my life—that art and the divine are inseparable. Since then, I have committed to living a life circumscribed by this union, to be a captive of beauty and enlightenment and creative revelation, whether it be found in the nave of a cathedral or at a listening station in a record shop.

"He who sings, prays twice," tradition holds that St.

OLDHAM COUNTY PUBLIC LIBRARY

Augustine said. It's a creed I know to be true whenever I hear the ambered voice of Patty Griffin or the tattered sounds of Billie Holiday, each time I listen to the Scottish folksinger Jean Redpath croon Robert Burns's "My Love Is Like a Red, Red Rose" in tones as clear as the River Dee.

This I believe—that in lifting our voices or pens we approach the divine, offering a prayer that rises through the air like incense.

JASON HOWARD *is the author of* A Few Honest Words *and coauthor of* Something's Rising. *His work has appeared in the* New York Times, The Nation, Sojourners, Paste, Equal Justice Magazine, *and the* Louisville Review, *and on NPR. A finalist for the 2013 Kentucky Literary Award, he was awarded the prestigious 2013 Al Smith Fellowship in Creative Nonfiction by the Kentucky Arts Council.*

# A Friendship with Nature

~

## Deborah Payne

I BELIEVE NATURE HAS AN IMPLICIT WAY OF BEING OUR friend.

I grew up in a neighborhood full of trees to climb, a creek that carried our small wooden boats, and tolerant neighbors who let us roam freely through their backyards. In those early years, nature became a companion and provider. I discovered how nice cool mud in the creek felt after running barefoot down gravel driveways and blacktopped streets. She extended a canopy of maple leaves over our heads when the summer sun was hot and harsh. We rested our bodies on her earth, our faces pressed on blankets of moss, cool and damp.

I also believe nature embraces us in our hour of need. I remember an evening when my adolescent heart was terribly upset. Though the details of the issue have long since slipped from memory, I still recall the embrace I received from the crooked old silver maple when I climbed up her branches and sobbed into her bark. The tree lifted me away and held me until I could stop the tears. Later, I asked my mother why she never came after me in my dramatic state.

"I saw you running to your tree," she replied. "I knew you were safe."

As I grew up, I maintained a respect for the environment that guided me into a career in environmental public health. I look at nature now through the lens of a microscope, observing the quality of water and its potential effect on our health. I consider things in parts per million and write reports on what excess mercury can do to the brain of a developing child. My thoughts are frequently consumed with environmental ethics, environmental law, and environmental epidemiology—categories that provide perspective on how the natural world works. I can get lost in the words and facts, policies and laws about emissions standards and whether they're adequately protective of human health.

But I believe once we establish a friendship with nature, it will never let us go. As I walk to work on brisk mornings, I hear a sudden lift in the wind passing through oak leaves that never fell last autumn. They shake and rattle as if to whisper hello, in a calm, reassuring rush.

At these moments when my mind is distracted from thoughts of work and deadlines, I remember the friend that supported and comforted me for so many long years. I feel the urge to protect this old, vulnerable friend in an effort to thank her for her companionship. I believe in loving your friends, whatever they are.

Deborah Payne *works in environmental public health advocacy focusing on issues related to energy and climate. She enjoys playing the fiddle and teaches lessons to students in her hometown of Berea, Kentucky.*

# You Are What You Believe

~

## SAMUEL R. GUARD,
### AS FEATURED IN THE 1950S SERIES

ACHIEVEMENT, LIKE HAPPINESS, COMES FROM WITHIN. YOU are what you believe. If you're a farmer, you can become a champion farmer if deep inside you will it so. My office is at the stock yards in Louisville, Kentucky. Farmers make my office a sort of headquarters—farmers from the rich river bottoms, from the hillside grasslands, future farmers, and gray-thatched farmers full of years. Oh, all kinds of farmers.

But this one was somebody. He loved to have his suit-case. It was full of corn, yellow-ear corn. He was a rugged but pleasant, broad-mouthed, and wrinkled man, wearing a store tie that persisted in coming unhooked. In one hand a suitcase and in the other hand a boy, a pleasant-looking country lad on the delicate side, his wide eyes full of wonderment with eagles and stars and things all over his coat lapels—emblems from Sunday school, the 4-H Club, the Junior Farm Girl.

"Mr. Sam," began the farmer, "I brought you some ears. I read what you said about wanting us American farmers to grow four billion bushels of corn a year instead of three billion bushels, so as to feed everybody at home and abroad, so as to get some beefsteak to put on the peace table, so as to stop inflation. This is my son, Cledith Raugh, Mr. Guard. I'm his 4-H leader at Burgin, Kentucky, way up in the mountains. I'm the school teacher up yonder, too. Cledith raised this corn on a measured acre and we thought you'd like to have some to decorate your office." With that, he opened the cheap suitcase and displayed the gleaming yellow corn. Was I tickled.

"How many bushels did, ah, Cledith raise on that measured acre?" I asked too casually. "I had 24,696 stocks on that acre, Mr. Guard. It weighed out 233 and two-tenths bushels," cried Cledith Raugh. I almost fell out of my chair. "Why that's more corn than any farmer, man or boy, in this whole United States grew on any solid acre of ground last year." "That must have been a mighty rich acre of ground," was all I could think of saying.

"Not especially," Mr. Jim Henry Raugh gave me to understand. He told me how he literally made that ground himself. "You see, when Pappy died he left me twenty-five acres, worth $10 an acre. I saved a little out of my teaching salary of $201 a month and bought seventy-five acres more, including this acre of Cledith's corn by the creek side. That was sixteen years ago."

Then he went on to explain how he took care of that land, year after year, enriching the soil and enlarging the yield—fifteen years from mountain land, poor as Job's turkey—to the highest solid acre of harvested corn on the globe. He became a champion farmer—the champion corn farmer of the U.S.A. He kept the faith. So I believe that achievement is within each of us. As the master said to the Pharisee, "The kingdom of God is within you." You are what you believe.

SAMUEL R. GUARD *worked in enterprises related to agriculture all of his life, and he was the owner and editor of* Breeder's Gazette, *a livestock farming magazine. Mr. Guard lived on a thirteen-acre farm at Anchorage, Kentucky, a farm he called Little Meadows since it resembled Daniel Boone's Great Meadows. Guard died in 1966.*

# One Diaper at a Time

◦

## Kristen Hands

I BELIEVE I AM CHANGING THE WORLD, ONE DIAPER AT A time. I have to believe this, or being home with my children would shake my sanity.

There was a time when my life was organized, my body moisturized. The freedoms of childfree adulthood went unappreciated. Now there's a new normal. I wear the same sweatpants and I constantly pick up toys. Days are full of sidewalk chalk, LEGOs, and the smell of grape cough syrup. The minutia of living with small children causes me to feel like my hours are on automatic replay: make food, serve food, clean up; make food, serve food, clean up. Where my life was once smooth jazz, now it's a cacophony of cartoons and Raffi on repeat. Some days I don't brush my teeth. Some days I feel invisible.

Before I became a mother, I thought parenting would be easy. I liked kids and was comfortable around them. I knew how to change a diaper and never wanted a life without children. But my firstborn brought a reality for which I was unprepared. My previous vision of motherhood came from the poetry of Mother's Day cards. In truth, my children cling to me like leeches, unrelenting bundles of need. It's difficult to find meaning amid the continuous knock-knock jokes and "Why? Why? Why?" The demands are constant; the crises are hourly. No, you cannot give my plants a haircut. No, your broccoli isn't poisonous. Yes, you must aim for the toilet. My sense of self, once confident and recognizable, is now at times fleeting and fragile. Gratefulness can be shamefully elusive.

Yet deep down, I know I have the most meaningful job in the world: raising children. I invest all that I know to be true and worthy into impressionable young lives and hope they forgive me when I fall short of what they deserve. While the days are long, the years are speeding by. I take my moments of beauty as they come: baking cookies together, finally finding a babysitter for date night, a stick-figured drawing of our family labeled "We aor happee." In these moments I see what I have, not what I lack. My carefully pruned former life is now a wild, overgrown garden bursting with color and scent. My life has never been so messy, or so beautiful.

I am a stay-at-home parent and I am thankful to have that choice. This bittersweet tether to the home gives me my sense of belonging and purpose. Though it is easily forgotten during the temper tantrums (both mine and theirs), this glorious tediousness is my calling. I am doing my best to raise children of integrity and compassion, and I trust that these values will pass on to future generations. This is what I offer to the world.

KRISTEN HANDS *is a Louisiana native who has called Lexington home for nearly twenty years. She joined a writing group at the Carnegie Center to have conversation with grownups during her kids' naptime. The basis for this essay originated there.*

# Small and Ordinary Actions

～

## Ngawang Gyatso

It was daybreak when I opened my eyes. Sunlight was beaming in the room through the window. After a quick wash I was handed a new set of clothes. It was my new look, my new monk robes. I never forget those words of wisdom my teacher told me. He said, "Like the robes you are about to wear with a bright color, remember your mind and heart should also generate the brightness of love and kindness to all without discrimination."

I was thirteen when I joined the monastery. Within the years as a monk, I have heard and come to know many generous and kind deeds that people have done for the global community. I have tried to contribute my thoughts and actions through different community groups and gatherings. It has been a wonderful experience. But still I always have this question in my mind. Is global peace possible? This thought would gain more momentum when I recalled the unrest and violence in several countries. That thought has changed and developed into a positive one with much hope and aspiration, due to a very good human being I met ten months ago.

I had newly arrived here from India. Every morning I would take my *mala* (rosary) and go for a walk to the beautiful Cherokee Park. One morning, I could see somebody bending down and trying to pick up something from the ground. In getting closer I saw a lady (maybe in her seventies) picking up an empty soda can from the street and putting it inside a big trash bag she was carrying in her right hand. When I reached closer I said, "Ma'am, do you need help?" She politely said, "No. Thank you for your kindness."

I once again asked her, "Are you waiting for the garbage truck?" With a long breath (she must have been working for quite some time) she said, "No, I am trying to collect and clean the trash which even the garbage truck leaves back. It makes the neighborhood look dirty." She had collected all those beer cans, papers, plastics, and even broken bottles.

While talking to her I came to know that she cleans the entire street. I introduced myself as a Buddhist monk. "Oh, you know," she said, "I am a Christian and I also follow the good thoughts shared by H.H. The Dalai Lama. Especially every morning when I come for this garbage collection, I remember his words of wisdom: 'No matter what is going on. No matter what is happening. No matter what is going on around you, never give up!'" I could see the joy in her face when she said, "I feel very happy in doing so, and my whole day passes very well after my cleaning." I realized that we don't have to form big gatherings and wait for someone or the government to act. If we have the motivation and commitment, we can serve the community, country, and the world in every small and ordinary [way] we can.

*At the time he wrote his* This I Believe *essay,* NGAWANG GYATSO *was a Tibetan Buddhist monk in residence at the Drepung Gomang Institute in Louisville. In 2009 he left the United States to help care for his family in India. Since then, he has left the Drepung Gomang Monastery and currently divides his time between India and Nepal.*

# A Lesson I Hold Dear

KARA GEBHART UHL

I BELIEVE I CAN BE BOTH HONEST AND KIND, EVEN WHEN THE two seem to contradict.

Honesty often throws kindness for a loop. From telling someone there's food in their teeth, all the way to telling someone you don't love them even though you know they love you—honest statements, although said with kind intentions, can often seem cruel.

I was sixteen years old, working at an amusement park, when I met Joe. He was older, had long, blond hair, and drove a motorcycle. The first time he called I smiled so hard my cheeks ached by the end of the conversation. He soon became my first boyfriend.

We dated the entire summer. By early fall he had said, "I love you." I said nothing. In the battle between kindness and honesty, honesty won.

In the months following our breakup, Joe left love notes on my bedroom windowsill. In college, he called twice. The first time we talked. The second time, he left a distraught voice mail. I returned his call and left a short message. I never heard from him again.

Several years later his sister called with news: Joe had committed suicide, months ago. Shortly before his death, his sister said, he had been diagnosed with bipolar disorder. Joe had written a few lines about me in his suicide note, but only now had she gathered the strength to call.

I thought about the first time Joe called, how my cheeks ached. The ache had returned—but this time, it was something much deeper. Not wanting to cry at work, I ran to my car and sobbed, both the finality of what he had done—and the fact that he had thought of me, even briefly, before he did it—sinking in. Once home, I reread his love letters to me. It was then I wanted so desperately to take back my silence, to tell him I loved him—not in a romantic sense, but in a you-deserve-to-live-a-long-life sense.

A few days later I went to a party on what would have been Joe's twenty-seventh birthday to celebrate his life. I met his family. I looked at old photos. I was intrigued to hear about the man he had become; we could have been great friends.

I hated myself for choosing honesty over kindness, for not writing more, for not calling more, for not doing more. I wasn't so bold as to think I could have fixed him. Rather, I was sad that I had to be unkind and tell him I didn't love him.

Several days later, worried I would never find peace, I reread what Joe wrote to me in his note: "How people should be . . . wonderful and I'm glad I had the time with her—still I have a wonderful feeling inside."

It was then I realized that Joe thought my honesty was kind. His words to me were his way of telling me so, his way of being honest—and kind—to me.

A year later, on what would have been Joe's twenty-eighth birthday, my husband and I put flowers by his grave. I thanked him for a lesson I'll always hold dear: I can be honest and still be kind.

KARA GEBHART UHL *is a freelance writer and editor who blogs about raising her daughter and twin boys at www.pleidesbee.com. Her essay "Apologies to the Parents I Judged Four Years Ago" was named one of* TIME *magazine's Top 10 Opinions of 2012.*

# In Celebration of Strangeness

SALLIE BINGHAM

I BELIEVE IN STRANGENESS.

One of the many blessings of my long life has been the frequent eruption of strangeness: people and events that startle or even frighten me, which I can't predict or control.

Like most of us, I usually seek the comfort of the familiar: old friends, old houses, and my routine.

I also depend on the comfort of work, which is true for many writers. After his wife's death, Leslie Stephen, Virginia Woolf's father, was devastated, as she describes it in *To the Lighthouse*: "Mr. Ramsey, stumbling along a passage one dark morning, stretched his arms out, but Mrs. Ramsey having died rather suddenly the night before, his arms, though stretched out, remained empty."

But in the heart of his bereavement, Leslie Stephen, as always, was at his desk at nine a.m. every day. I don't know what he wrote, but that doesn't matter. He soothed himself with the familiar in the face of the strangeness of death.

I was fortunate in my childhood for many reasons, most of all for the unpredictable appearance of strange relatives, usually at Sunday lunch. Their strangeness was obvious but never labeled or explained, as it would be today. We children knew we were expected to be polite; I resented the necessity.

One Sunday visitor was an ancient cousin, red-faced, wattled, and almost stone deaf. His passion was opera, and he played his red vinyl records at top volume after lunch.

Another, when we visited her, laughed with frightening intensity; her lipstick was smeared from her top lip to her nose, and she was noisily affectionate.

A third strange one was never mentioned. Around dinnertime, in that dim old house in Asheville, he would appear at the door to his private staircase, in robe and slippers, and disappear silently into the kitchen. No one explained who he was or what he was doing; he lived out his life on the top floor. When I visited the old house right before it was demolished, the floor of his room was several inches deep in letters from women who had loved him—another strange and puzzling fact.

These blessed strangers erupt into my present life, too. Last night, at an elegant dinner given by a friend, I heard the telephone ringing insistently behind a closed door, followed by shrieks of laughter. "Well, thank you," one of the guests said. No one asked our host for an explanation.

Recognizing the strangeness in all human beings, usually deeply hidden and smoothed over, has helped me to recognize, and accept, my own strangeness.

Perhaps one day I'll call it mystery and see its appearance as a manifestation of grace.

SALLIE BINGHAM *began writing as a child and published her first novel two years after graduating from Radcliffe College. Since then she has published a memoir,* Passion and Prejudice, *four additional novels, and five collections of short stories. A new nonfiction book,* The Blue Box: Three Lives in Letters, *will be published by Sarabande Books in 2014. She is currently working on a biography of Doris Duke, to be published by Farrar, Straus and Giroux.*

# Helping Myself

~~~

## WILLIAM KELLER,
### AS FEATURED IN THE 1950S SERIES

I BELIEVE THAT MY PERSONAL PHILOSOPHY OF LIVING WAS pretty much blueprinted for me by my father, who was a physician engaged in general practice in our town. You know the type: babies, boils, and broken bones. From him I got most of my basic beliefs. Sickness and suffering are great levelers and tend to equalize many differences, such as religious, financial, and social.

I believe the Golden Rule pays off the greatest dividends in human relationships. I believe that ambition is an excellent attribute if the aim is an obtainable goal. I believe that aside from those catastrophic misfortunes which sometimes hit all of us, people create most of their own problems. I believe that we can do a great deal for people without ever really helping them.

Now as a psychiatrist, I have seen and talked to thousands of people who were having difficulties. I have been particularly fortunate, having been born, reared, and educated in the same place where I teach and practice psychiatry. This has given me the opportunity to see many of the same people over a long period of time in the actual process of living, with all the happiness and unhappiness involved therein. Out of these experiences has come a strengthening of my earlier beliefs and teachings. Illness, trouble, and pain force one—with humility—to recognize a common heritage of humanity.

Coming from a city with a Southern past and having had a grandfather who fought for the Confederacy, it was important for me to learn that colored people can get just as sick as anybody, and that in combating anemia, Negro blood is just as effective as white blood.

The Golden Rule precludes selfishness, but I see so many people who have never learned its basic principle. The simple rule of treating other people as you would like to be treated can bring infinite happiness and tremendous satisfactions. I see many patients who have suffered from too much ambition and have tried frustratedly to own the shoe factory rather than content themselves with being the best cobbler in the entire area—this in spite of the fact that almost everybody wears shoes.

Most people seem to make their own little troubles by worrying, fretting, and stewing about highly improbable, disastrous happenings. It is a rare experience for a psychiatrist to see something actually come to pass that a patient has been worrying about. Once, between halves of a high school football game, our coach was berating the team for fumbling—I was the waterboy. When one of the players protested that the other team was getting all the breaks, the coach replied, "The best team forces the breaks." And I believe I see many people who do not recover fumbles and who are unhappy about some other person who they believe is getting the breaks.

Now although my father died when I was relatively young, he taught me the value and satisfaction of helping myself. And I feel I see many instances where an effort is made to help people, but too often there is little effort made to help people help themselves. Now these things I believe, partly because they were taught me and have allowed me to live a full and happy life, and partly because as a psychiatrist I see many unhappy people who have not been able to accept them.

*Born in 1907 in Louisville's Portland neighborhood,* DR. WILLIAM "BILLY" KELLER *became one of the city's most prominent medical authorities. At the University of Louisville, Keller chaired the Medical School's Department of Psychiatry and Behavioral Sciences from 1964 to 1973. Keller was also notably passionate about highway safety and was one of America's first advocates for automobile seat belt laws. Keller died in Louisville in 1990.*

# Rejecting War, Embracing Nonviolence

MICHAEL WESTMORELAND-WHITE

I CAME FROM A FAMILY IN WHICH A TERM (NOT A CAREER) OF military service was traditional. It was assumed that when I turned eighteen, I would enlist in a branch of the US military for a "hitch" before returning to civilian life. So I did, joining the US Army in 1980.

However, on my way to basic training, a friend of mine from high school challenged me to memorize the Sermon on the Mount. So I spent my days learning to be a soldier and my "spare time" reading and memorizing the teachings of Jesus in Matthew 5:7, with the blessing on peacemakers and commands to love enemies, to turn the other cheek, etc. This set up cognitive dissonance that came to a head about a year later while I was stationed in Heidelberg, Germany. I encountered some German Christians deeply committed to peacemaking. Convinced that this was also the route I was called to follow, I applied for a discharge as a conscientious objector (CO). It took me about a year, but I was granted an honorable CO discharge.

That changed the entire direction of my life. For the last thirty-one years, I have been a peace activist. I have traveled to Nicaragua twice (1983 and '84) with Witness for Peace, working to prevent a US invasion and collecting evidence on the depravities of the Contras for Congress. I have been involved in resisting nuclear weapons, in attempting to close the School of the Americas, and in numerous marches and protests against the US invasion of Iraq.

At a time of global terrorism, "preemptive wars" and the accumulation of huge arsenals by the United States, I have found my convictions on nonviolence reinforced. Clearly violence and war are not helping to do anything productive in the world. Active nonviolence and peacemaking can help forge a more just and peaceful world and have made great strides against overwhelming odds.

My commitment to nonviolence grew out of my developing faith as a Christian, but I don't want to give the impression that only Christians can have such a commitment. In the world's great religions in our day, there seems to be a debate between those committed to "redemptive violence," whereby they hope to rid the world of evil by killing all the evil people they can find, and those committed to a different way—a way of peacemaking and nonviolent struggle. Our time is a time of choosing: I stand with the nonviolent ones—nonviolent Buddhists, Muslims, Jews, Hindus, Christians, and those whose commitment to nonviolence is itself a form of spirituality.

I believe that means and ends must cohere. People who support military force often do so for good reasons and hope to achieve good ends: the defense of a democracy or the liberation of a people from tyranny, for example. But the means chosen—guns, drones, bombs, and other forms of military violence—subvert the ends they hope to achieve. The path of nonviolence seeks ends that flow from the means we use to achieve them. I believe it to be the path toward a more humane future.

---

MICHAEL L. WESTMORELAND-WHITE, PhD, *lives in Louisville and teaches courses related to philosophy, ethics, and religion, including courses on war and peacemaking, on a part-time basis at several colleges and universities in the Louisville and southern Indiana area. He is also a freelance writer on these topics. At the time this essay was written in 2005, Dr. Westmoreland-White was executive director of Every Church a Peace Church, and he remains active on the boards of several activist peace groups, including the Baptist Peace Fellowship of North America, the Fellowship of Reconciliation, and the War Resisters League.*

## Somebody to Lean On

COLE DOWDY

YOU KNOW THE OLD SONG "LEAN ON ME," BY BILL WITH-ers? What a simple song that to any average person is just another tune on the radio. But to me, that song emphasizes a belief that I've had for most of my life. I believe that everyone needs someone to depend on—to know they're there for you no matter what.

For me, I rely on my identical twin brother, Tanner. Yes, we have the same DNA, so in that respect we have as close a bond as you can get. The only things that make me different from him are my personal experiences. But despite the close genetic bond, I think we share a brotherhood that is different from all other brothers. We go through the same things, think the same way, and even get on each other's nerves, only because we can't be separated. Something as small as shooting hoops without him feels odd. Now I don't mean to sound mushy, but I don't know how else to put it. Because of our bond, we need each other, depend on each other.

I can recall certain times when we needed each other, like running a hard cross-country meet, or even harder times like going to a new middle school with completely new friends. But there is one specific time in my life when I made the connection that everyone needs someone to lean on when life gets hard, and for me, that one person is my brother.

The moment I realized this was after my bone graft surgery. Tanner and I were born with cleft lip and palate, and this was one of many procedures we needed to have done. We were both getting the surgery done on the same day. After the surgery, I was aching in pain all over, had horrible nausea, and was sick of the antiseptic smell of the hospital room. I was really ready to go home. My thinking was in and out; I was sleeping a lot and eating little. I was just feeling pretty alone when my mind told me to look to my left, to my bedside. There, I saw Tanner, all sick and tired, just like me. He was going through everything I was. He knew just how I felt. I sat there and realized that this is why we are so close. No one on earth knows me as well as he does.

Without him, I felt alone. But with him there, I knew I could get through it.

Right then, I came to believe that everyone needs someone to lean on. Whether it's a mother and a child, two inseparable friends, a husband and a wife, or even a dog and its owner. Everyone needs someone to rely on in this life. We cannot live life alone.

Is it a simple belief, like in Bill Withers's song? Yes. Is it powerful? More than powerful, it's true. I believe we all need somebody to lean on.

COLE DOWDY *wrote this essay for an assignment by his eighth-grade teacher at East Oldham Middle School. He now goes to South Oldham High School, where he enjoys running cross-country and track. Mr. Dowdy lives with his family in Crestwood, Kentucky, a small town just outside of Louisville.*

# Celebrating Our Lives Together

SUZY SZASZ PALMER

I BELIEVE IN MEMORIAL SERVICES. I'VE LEARNED THIS THE hard way—from all the times someone close to me has died, and the obituary informed me: "There will be no memorial service."

I remember the first time I felt this way. It was during the summer of 1990, just days after my thirty-fifth birthday. My grandmother, "Anya," as my father called her in his native Hungarian, had died a few months shy of ninety-six. Widowed for almost thirty years, she had built an enormous circle of friends and had a rich life. Active well into her eighties, Anya had grown increasingly frail prior to her death, but her mind remained sharp and her spirits good.

By ninety, she had given up swimming regularly at the YWCA but kept volunteering at the Red Cross, playing bridge, and baking tortes with layer upon layer of chocolate cake and whipped cream. Above all, she was strong-minded: Anya wanted no memorial service. My father, sister, and I abided by her wishes, but it has always bothered me. When my father died last fall, I knew instinctively he also wanted no memorial service, which again left family and friends asking, "why not?"

Now in my late fifties, I've witnessed the death of too many acquaintances from a variety of insidious diseases. And too often, the last wish of my dying friend included those same instructions—no memorial service—leaving those of us who loved them to mourn their deaths alone instead of celebrating their lives together.

I admit I think about the frailty of life more than most: I nearly died at the age of thirteen, and have lived with lupus ever since. I suffered a severe "flare" fifteen years later that once again almost killed me, but instead forced me to stop working for a year and learn how to walk again, and it reduced my already short stature by three inches.

My lupus has been mostly stable since then, but these events have left an indelible mark on my soul. I try nonetheless to heed the words of poet Christian Wiman, who says, "The greatest tragedy of human existence is not to live in time, in both senses of that phrase."

Yet I still pondered after hearing the news of another death: why can't we understand that even though the act of dying is inevitably individual, death, like life, has a broader social meaning? Why don't we grasp that death must not only be shared but embraced by the living? Have we become so secular a society that we're afraid to observe rituals? Or is it that these rituals are uncomfortable reminders of our own mortality?

When I die, I promise not to cheat my friends and family out of the chance to get together with me one last time: to share short jokes, eat Swiss chocolate truffles, and drink French champagne. If I've forgotten something, I leave it to them to add what each remembers best about me. But mostly I want them to tell someone they love: "Have a memorial service for me."

---

*Originally from upstate New York,* SUZY SZASZ PALMER *was an associate dean at the University of Louisville libraries and is now dean of the library at Longwood University in Farmville, Virginia. She has written a book on living with lupus and is an avid cook and knitter. She lives with her husband in Richmond and Farmville.*

# Antidote for War

~

## Ben Lucien Burman,
### AS FEATURED IN THE 1950S SERIES

I BECAME A PHILOSOPHER EARLY. I HAD TO BECOME A PHILOS-
opher. I was rather badly wounded in the First World War
at Soissons, France, when I was twenty-two, and as a result,
I was flat on my back for a long time. It was either get a
philosophy, or crack up. My code of living is simple. It con-
sists of three parts: 1) never be cruel; 2) always be artistic;
3) never lose your sense of humor.

Number one, I don't believe, requires much explanation.
"Never be cruel" means, of course, always be kind. I believe
that kindness is the natural human instinct, not cruelty.
I have no illusions about humanity. I know its faults, its

frequent blindness, its capacity for making terrible mistakes. But my work as a writer takes me among all kinds of men and women, often the very rough and the very poor. Everywhere, I have found generosity and nobility—men who would have gladly given their lives for me, because I had done them some slight kindness. The vast majority of human beings will do the basically good thing if they are given half a chance.

By the second point in my code, "always be artistic," I mean that whatever I do, I try to do with as much grace as possible. If I write a book, I want to make it as beautiful as I can. If I were a shoemaker, I would want to make shoes the same way, as perfect as possible. In our madly commercialized and mechanized world, we have lost our sense of the beautiful. I believe we need beauty in our lives just as much as we need food on our dining room tables. A world where beauty flourishes is a happy world, a world at peace.

The third part of my code, as I said earlier, is "never lose your sense of humor." I don't like pomposity; I don't like stuffed shirts. I'm glad I was born in a small town. It's a wonderful antidote for smugness.

I remember years ago when I had a little success in New York with one of my first novels, there was the usual round of autograph parties and literary lunches, and I was feeling rather pleased with myself. About this time, I happened to go back to my hometown in Kentucky, and I saw an old fellow I'd known as a boy standing on the street corner. He looked me up and down a long time and remarked lazily, "How are yah, Benny? You been away a while, ain't yah? Yah still teachin' school?" That reduced life to its proper proportions.

I was over in Germany not long ago in the ruins of Berlin, and a reporter asked me to give his paper a thought for the day. That was a bit of an order for me, who had been in two wars against the Germans and had very definite physical souvenirs from both. I reflected on what I could tell the Germans under these circumstances, and then I wrote, "When all the peoples of the world remember to laugh, particularly at themselves, there will be no more dictators and no more wars."

BEN LUCIEN BURMAN *was an American author and journalist born in Covington, Kentucky, and educated at Harvard University. Burman wrote twenty-two books, including the bestselling* Catfish Bend *series about life in a fictitious Mississippi River town. Several of his books became movies, which included* Steamboat Round the Bend, *starring Will Rogers. Burman died from a stroke in 1984 at the age of eighty-eight.*

# The Power of Parenthood

~

## Andrea Coleman

On a bright spring day nine years ago, I went shopping at a popular store in my small hometown. It was a chore I'd completed hundreds of times before, but this trip was special: it was the first time I took my baby daughter with me.

Kendall was a preemie who, despite being three months old, looked like a newborn. Still, she was alert and active. As happens with babies, alert and active quickly became bored and restless. I picked her up, began the swaying motion every mom knows will calm a fussy infant, and continued shopping.

An older woman stopped and remarked on what a pretty baby Kendall was. She stroked the soft cheek resting on my shoulder and smiled when Kendall snuffled out a tiny snore. As I turned to settle my sleeping daughter back into her carrier, the woman said, "Poor dear, are your hands still too swollen for your wedding band?"

"I'm not married, ma'am," I replied with the respect I was raised to offer my elders.

"Well! You certainly don't look like that kind of girl."

I looked at her over my shoulder, not entirely certain she was serious, only to see her stomp off with an air of righteous indignation. I glanced down at my child, feeling a messy tangle of emotions: surprise, hurt, anger, and, though I hate to admit it, a stab of embarrassment. Until that moment, the idea of anyone assuming that "single mother" and "good mother" were mutually exclusive terms had never occurred to me. As I finished shopping, the woman's words echoed in my mind.

"You certainly don't look like that kind of girl."

As I thought about it, though, I decided to spin her statement in a positive way. Yes, I was a single mother. I was also a good mother. The negative emotions pulling at me began to fade away.

Raising a child alone is as rewarding as it is terrifying, and while I admit it might not be an ideal situation for anyone, it's also not the worst circumstance one can be in. I left an unhealthy relationship when I learned I was pregnant. I would never subject my child to the pain that relationship brought me. I made a conscious decision to be a single mother. It was the right decision, even if some people don't agree with it.

I believe single parents have to be strong, determined, and able to depend on themselves. We must be both mother and father, and undertake both roles with equal commitment. I am now married to a man who is a wonderful father to Kendall, but I wouldn't change the early years when it was just my daughter and me, because I know wedding bands and marriage vows are no guarantee a woman will be a good mother, just as the lack of them is no sign she isn't.

I believe in the power of parenthood—even when the power comes from a solitary source.

ANDREA COLEMAN *teaches language arts at Johnson County Middle School in Paintsville, Kentucky. She also writes fiction for young adults and is pursuing her MFA in creative writing. Her greatest accomplishment in life, Kendall James, is the inspiration for everything she does.*

# Work Is the Sweetening of Life

～

## KATHERINE HOENIG BOTTIGHEIMER,
### AS FEATURED IN THE 1950S SERIES

THE SUMMER I WAS TEN, I WAS ALLOWED TO VISIT IN A nearby city where a number of my elderly relatives lived. Among these was Cousin Theresa, an oldish widow who lived with her middle-aged spinster daughters. In the course of my duties as a member of the younger generation, I was required to visit Cousin Theresa for an hour or more at frequent intervals. I found her always knitting, crocheting, or sewing, and always she urged me to let her teach me her skills so that I too could pass idle hours profitably.

I based my refusal of these offers on the fact that the articles on which Cousin Theresa expended her time were neither attractive in color nor interesting in design. I had wanted to make gaily colored scarves, mittens, or ruffled petticoats.

At that point, Cousin Theresa revealed to me a philosophy, which—while it did little to change my attitude at the time—apparently made a lasting impression on my later behavior. "Work is the sweetening of life," she said. "You are a plain child and, as far as one can now determine, not endowed with any outstanding talents. You must learn quite early how much your happiness will depend on the useful services you will perform. These articles you call ugly and uninteresting are used by children in orphanages, old people in pauper homes, and patients in charity hospitals. My satisfaction lies in having performed a needed service, one that was at hand and also one which many others would disdain. I have found that to turn one's back on a job to be done—no matter how drab—is a fatal error. Work in and of itself is not only healing, it is infinitely sweet."

I am sure that these words did not create in me a firm and instantaneous resolve to go and do likewise. I was convinced that Cousin Theresa was more than a little queer, and that sooner or later the family would have to do something about her.

When I was asked to set forth what I believe, I found it necessary to take a good, long look at what I do. For what one does, somehow, expresses most sincerely what one believes. Imagine my own amazement when I discovered that nearly all my adult years had been devoted to much the same kind of activity in which Cousin Theresa found her satisfaction. Of course, I have not fashioned utilitarian garments; mechanized production has long since removed the need for the handmade items of the far-removed day. Like the responsibilities I carry in my family and in my household, my assignments during my long years in the League of Women Voters have not been glamorous. I have always been in the labor battalions where the heartbreaking and the backbreaking jobs are done. I have, albeit unwittingly, turned my heart, my mind, and my physical energy to jobs at hand.

Through the frightening years before and during World War II, through the hazards of childrearing, of watching loved ones sicken and die, of personal illness whose very presence carried emotional threats, and now again in the frustration and near despair produced by the state of the world today, I have found that the application of elbow grease and a relative peace of mind have much to do with each other. The quotation from Ecclesiastes, "Whatsoever thy hand findest to do, do it with thy might," has come alive for me.

*Born in 1906 in Kentucky,* KATHERINE HOENIG BOT-TIGHEIMER *spent the time and energy of her adult life as a community activist involved in a wide array of causes and organizations, including the Girl Scouts, the Temple Sisterhood, and the Louisville chapter of the League of Women Voters, of which Bottigheimer served as president from 1955 to 1957. Regarded both as a diligent activist and devoted housewife and mother, Bottigheimer died in Louisville in 2001 at age ninety-four.*

# My Black Mother

~

## BARBARA SIMMS CARPENTER

I AM A WHITE WOMAN IN MY MID-SIXTIES. AS A YOUNG GIRL, I didn't know much about the Great Depression, except that our family lost many material things, including our house and car. When I was nearly four years old, my mother "left" me to go to work, and that is when I met Nellie.

Nellie was a petite black woman who was very tidy and fastidious and always dressed nicely. I thought she must be far wealthier than we, as there was a certain proper air about her, and I reckoned that the very small gold earrings in her pierced earlobes were a clincher for her status. She was a reserved woman who meant business when she spoke. I saw her as having a stern demeanor, but she was also caring.

My older sister and two brothers were already of school age, so for one full year, I was alone with Nellie from the time my mother left in the morning to the time my mother returned home.

The next school year I started kindergarten. Each day Nellie walked me to school and was there to meet me when school was out at noon. She gently held my hand as we silently walked home. By now I felt more comfortable with her as our routine was firmly established. I did, however, notice one curious fact and so I asked my mother, "Why am I the only one with a black mother?" My mother then explained that she was still my only mother and that Nellie was simply taking care of me while she worked during the day. I felt reassured that I had not been abandoned and that I still only had one mother.

As children are wont to do, I began learning from the other children at school, picking up on their sayings and mimicking what I would hear. One afternoon while Nellie brushed my hair, I very proudly recited a rhyme I had just learned: "eeny, meeny, miney, moe, crack a nigger on the toe. If he hollers, make him pay fifty dollars every day."

The words were meaningless to me; I was just proud of my memorization. Nellie said, "What did you say?" I naively repeated the rhyme. Again, she asked the same question. By now I sensed something was wrong but I didn't know what. I repeated the rhyme a little more slowly, thinking as I went along, indeed, wondering what I had said that caused Nellie's strong reaction. As I reached the words "crack a nigger," I said them out loud but then stopped. I felt embarrassed as I recognized it was the derogatory word "nigger" that was hurtful. As my back was to Nellie, she stepped to my side and with a hard stare she icily said, "Don't ever say that again." I sat quietly, digesting what had transpired. I felt a bit scared, and I also felt bad that I had hurt her feelings.

It was that short dialogue between the two of us that was my first lesson in racism. It was also the first time I understood how words could hurt another. My lesson was learned not by any diatribe or lecture. Nellie was wise. She made me aware of my words by calling me to think . . . to think of what I was saying and how it was affecting her.

Nellie was as steady and dependable as the sunrise. She continued to care for me and worked with my family until I entered the fourth grade. I am forever grateful for her good care of me.

I believe I was profoundly influenced by my black mother, who taught me the importance of thinking and of weighing my words. I do not know where Nellie went after leaving our family. I know that, forever, she is in my memory, and is still a part of my heart and being.

BARBARA SIMMS CARPENTER *is a native Louisvillian. She has a BA degree from Ursuline/Bellarmine University and a master's degree from Western Kentucky University. Ms. Carpenter served in the Peace Corps from 1962 to 1964 in Arequipa, Peru, was a social worker for four years with the City of Louisville, and is a retired EAP counselor. Married to Thomas D. Carpenter, she has five daughters and nine grandchildren.*

# *You Don't Know What You Don't Know*

~

## Owsley Brown III

I BELIEVE THAT YOU DON'T KNOW WHAT YOU DON'T KNOW, until . . . you come to know it. I am amazed at how much there is to learn and what a tremendous capacity we have to learn if we connect with our naturally curious and open minds and hearts.

This idea came to me as I looked into my spiritual life and toward teachings on compassion. My personal inquiry began as a young boy growing up in Kentucky. My parents wanted me to "have faith," and my mother nurtured this in me by way of a church-going life through Roman Catholicism. One of the people she admired most from that world was Kentucky's adopted son, Thomas Merton, the great twentieth-century contemplative and Catholic monk. Through her, I too became enamored with Merton.

Merton was a prolific writer, and as a young man he inspired me enormously by way of his inspiring and profound ideas. What touched me most was his pointing out the amazing concept of altruism best expressed through the "Bodhisattva ideal" of Mahayana Buddhism. I began to look further into this area, and big questions arose for me from this inquiry. What if we really *did* put others before ourselves? What would the world look like then? Is there a connection between true freedom and the hard work of being altruistic? And could this work lead to a more honest, refined, and overall beneficial way of relating to all aspects of life?

Almost half a century after Merton's death, I find myself still engaged with these questions and with the issues of compassion and altruism as they are being discussed in my hometown of Louisville.

Recently I interviewed Louisville's mayor, Greg Fischer, before a group of city leaders. The purpose of the meeting was to discuss current expressions of compassion in the city. During the interview, we all were challenged by one of the mayor's supporters to go beyond rhetoric—to show how compassion can create jobs and bring hope back to places where despair now reigns. It was a difficult moment for me. This challenge made me realize that it is easy to want compassion but hard to embody compassion. I wondered how a concept as attractive as compassion could be made real in vulnerable parts of our city—places with problems I might not have understood, or even considered.

But then I realized that accessing real compassion, rather than something that made me *feel* good, was the whole point! In an effort to figure out what authentic compassion was, I thought back to the key spiritual teachings I had studied through Merton, and I was reminded that the idea is to be open to what *is* rather than what I want. And I believe that the hard work of compassion really is about the uncomfortable idea of living life not on one's *own* terms, but rather in a way that will best serve others. I believe this is the gateway to authentic compassion. And I hope to know this in my own life, and to share this with as many others as I possibly can.

OWSLEY BROWN III, *a University of Virginia graduate, aligns his entrepreneurial spirit among the fields of documentary filmmaking, sustainable winemaking, and philanthropy. His current film project, Ke Kontan, is a profile of a music school in Haiti both before and after a devastating earthquake. A Louisville native, he currently lives in San Francisco with his wife and three children.*

# Dawn in the Garden

∽

## Nana Lampton

This morning I remembered to turn off the sprinkler in the garden. I meant to turn it off by sunset last evening. As I padded back to the house at dawn, through the phlox, and calla lilies, yellow dahlias, lavender, I observed how I was moving—forward. I have two eyes directed ahead of me, feet designed to employ hips and knees, arms that help propel me forward. We manipulate all those bones and muscles to progress in a line to the next destination. We do not move in circles, and generally not backwards.

Just now I have directed the hay harvest, ridden a horse, briefly watched the news, jumped in the pond, dressed for the office, and now I sit at my desk. I have figured out a way to drive home in forty minutes in the company of a businesswoman who has little spare time. She will drive out and back with me so I can let out the dogs, and make it back to town in time for dinner. We will have the visit she has been requesting, as her husband just died of cancer.

We each radiate circles. We make interlocking rounds to lap into each other. I offer my problems to my friends, and they offer theirs to me, as if we knew exactly what to do about each other's full platters.

We put heel first, our wide toes making a platform for the rest of the structure. Proceeding along a linear path our eyes travel ahead. To evolve, I think we need to imagine ways to encircle, if only by including others in our walking path.

For a while, I have been involved with the country of Morocco. What impresses me about it is that the country has always taken in the foreigners who need a place to light—Jews from Europe, Muslims from their home in Spain, Germans, French, English, Middle Eastern families, Berbers for six thousand years. The country survives between the Atlas Mountains and the sea, with the desert at its feet. I understand its intent is to include for the sake of richness—food, music, language, thinking. For a good eight hundred years the country has sought this role. Diversity reigns with the king. It is inspiring to look down on the Phoenician harbor in Rabat. Now, Rachad Bouhlal, the ambassador from Morocco to the United States, is making the links between Kentucky and Morocco—bourbon, Thoroughbred horses, airplanes, agriculture, music, health care, and tourism. Bring it all together: <u>our</u> music to the Fez music festival, their couscous to Kentucky. When I was there at the harbor in Rabat, at a great celebration, we walked on beautiful carpets through an arch, with girls in festive dresses throwing rose petals as we entered. Traditional musicians played flutes, guitars, and tambourines while the women danced. I joined them. At least one can go circular in a dance, holding hands, going over and under arms held up and down. You whirl with the music. They were joined in a movement quite parallel to my early morning walk through the garden: thousands of years of progress, slowly, surely, one step at a time. This, I believe, is the course of life, focused and yet ever moving forward.

Even if I have the basic structure we humans share—two feet forward, eyes ahead, hips going frontwards—I can open arms to greet people. Or open arms to the dawn, or to the great oak, the *axis mundi* that carries our thoughts up the trunk out the branches to the cosmos. I can carry a tray to my friends who sit in rocking chairs on the porch. I can give them plates and forks, napkins and glasses for apple pie and iced tea, or chocolate pudding and brandy, or berries and cream with coffee. I believe that anything I give is to reach past a line into their circle.

NANA LAMPTON *leads a Louisville-based company her grandfather founded in 1906. She attended Wellesley College, University of Virginia, and Spalding University. An honorary consul to the Kingdom of Morocco, she is an active businesswoman whose interests include community development, historic preservation, land conservation, and the arts. A published poet and artist, she lives on a farm in Goshen, Kentucky.*

# The Answer Is in Rural America

GERRY ROLL

I BELIEVE THE REAL PROMISE AND HOPE FOR OUR FUTURE AS a country lie in rural America. Where I live, like most of America, is still rural. Our coal fields, our farmland, our deserts, and our prairies are beautiful, wide open spaces where things still grow and land has more intrinsic value than simply what you can build on it. I believe the true heart of America is rural.

A person can still breathe in rural America, and I don't mean just taking in air. There is real space for everyone. We all fit comfortably. I believe that too many people crammed into a small space just breeds irritation—that doesn't happen where I live.

And people are still nice to each other here—there's no anonymity in a small town. I can be hateful toward somebody today, but it's a sure bet I'm going to see them tomorrow, so I'm at least going to think about it before I lash out in a rage. In these times of war, anxiety, and distrust, I believe we need to do more stopping and thinking, and less snarling and snapping. We need to get used to being accountable to each other again.

Sure, there's not a lot of hip-hop and hype where I live. We don't have flashing neon lights, huge malls, or much of the stereotypical urban nightlife, but we have plenty to do. We sit on the front porch, and we talk to each other. We eat together. We play ball and go to various houses of worship where everybody knows each other's first name. There's a real sense of civility in rural America. And I sense we are losing more and more of that civility with every person we add to an overcrowded metropolitan area every day.

As I watch people flood into New York and Los Angeles and hear how all of our cities are beginning to run out of water and land and clean air, I have to wonder—what is everybody looking for? My children believe they have to leave this small town to make more money. I believe they should stay here and make more of a life.

Ironically, the more people that come to know the value and meaning of rural life, the less rural my town will become. But it's a risk I'm willing to take. It's a risk I believe rural America will take, and the gift rural people will make, to restore peace and real prosperity to our nation.

GERRY ROLL *is the director of the Foundation for Appalachian Kentucky in Chavies. She was born in West Palm Beach, Florida, and moved from there to Hazard, Kentucky, with her two boys in 1991 in order to live a more peaceful, meaningful life.*

# The Holy Grail of Peaceful Coexistence

⟳

## Djenita Pasic

I BELIEVE IN NOT BEING DEFINED BY RELIGION. TO ME, RELI-
gion is just like communism—a beautiful, noble idea that
we are all created equal, which does not work too well in
practice.

Do not take me wrong: I am in favor of all the basic
premises taught by all religions. But I have a serious problem with how all religions treat "others," those who do not
belong, in practice.

I was born into a Muslim family but I was raised in a
communist, or rather socialist, country of Yugoslavia. With
no religious practice or training in our upbringing, but with
plenty of education and communist propaganda, I believed

in my country, our way of life, our mutual, intermixed, and tolerant religious heritage without ever even thinking it may not last forever.

I suffered for the people in Beirut or Jerusalem and their constant wars because I believed we, in Yugoslavia, were different. I believed that we may have found the holy grail of peaceful coexistence, and I was very proud of it.

But then the war came to our country, and this beautiful dream fell apart. All of a sudden we were told that we were different among ourselves, that our religions now defined who we were, and that we no longer had our communist common denominator. All of a sudden I became just another Muslim who could get killed, tortured, or raped just because of my religion, which I never even practiced! Two hundred thousand dead and one million displaced Bosnian Muslims later, I realized it was time for change. I could no longer bury my head in the sand; I had to accept reality as is. I may have gone through the trauma of war and resettlement not visibly scathed, but I knew better.

Because of the experience of war in my home country, I "became" very much a Muslim, but I am also still a "communist" at heart. I know this may be the worst possible combination in the United States, but I am no terrorist or anarchist. I am more of an existentialist and a pacifist, happy with my choices. And I want to promote my European, intermixed, and tolerant heritage, which is still in the hearts and minds of my family and friends in my home city of Sarajevo.

Because of genocide over Muslims in Bosnia and Herzegovina, I feel compelled and obliged to belong, to defend and represent hundreds of thousands of victims of this incomprehensible war. I believe in giving those victims my voice. My allegiance is with "my" Muslim people but not at the expense of others. I have seen and experienced the holy grail of peaceful coexistence, and I will pursue it forever.

However, while I am Muslim, I refuse to be defined by religion. This, I believe.

Attorney DJENITA PASIC and her family settled in Louisville, Kentucky, as Serbian forces laid siege to her hometown of Sarajevo for over three years. Pasic now is a partner at the law firm of Kahloon, Pasic & Lewis. She remains committed to education, peacemaking, and civil liberty issues.

# The Way of Silence

DIANNE APRILE

I BELIEVE IN SILENCE. IN ITS POWER AND ITS PERSUASION.

I believe that the act of saying nothing often—no, *usually*—speaks louder than words ever could.

Monks know this. From Thích Nhất Hạnh to Thomas Merton to the Dalai Lama, monks know and understand the deeply felt significance of the unspoken.

Poets know it, too. E. E. Cummings said: *Silence is a looking bird.* Not a singing bird. A looking bird. A bird observing, noticing, listening. Being. Here. Now.

But so do we ordinary women and men know the profound power of silence. Intuitively, we know it.

Consider the wordless communication between mother

and newborn at her breast. Or the tacit tête-à-tête that exists in a hospital room where the dying lies in bed and the friend sits, silent, at her side.

I believe in the authority of silence.

What if governments, rather than reacting with statements and decrees, observed silence—briefly but routinely—at times of crisis? What if we, the citizens, stopped to quietly reflect on the day's news, rather than jumping into the fray with rushed judgments and verbal crossfire?

Silence has its own eloquence.

Think of the times you dissolved a disagreement by not giving expression to the negative emotions it stirred in you.

I believe silence is a way of affirming life, even in a democracy—which, at its heart, is a public conversation. Let's not forget: conversation implies alternating patterns of listening and talking—equal parts silence and speech.

Imagine an election campaign where no one spoke unless they had something to say. Where silence was imposed for, oh, a calming few minutes after a debate or a misspoken word—so we could meditate on what was said (and *not* said) before grumbling hordes of commentators burst forth to tell *us* what *we* heard.

Think of silence in music, the pause—that empty moment, a bridge between what came before and what is to come. A moment of awareness of the present, with a nod to the past and an ear turned to the future.

Silence, Mary Oliver says, gives poetry its rhythm and music. So too our lives need silence—patches of nothingness, ellipses of emptiness, to inform the drumbeat of our days. And of our duties.

Think of the heroes and movements that used silence to change the world. Silence, as in the refusal to act in bad faith, to follow immoral orders, to go along with wars and poverty and discrimination and the earth's destruction.

I believe in silence, in its yearning for wholeness, its desire to close the breach, its urge to unite what's come asunder.

Silence too often gets a bad rap. It's not apathy or surrender. It's not looking the other way.

Likewise, speaking is not necessarily speaking out. Sometimes words get in the way of reconciliation. They convey noise, not knowledge.

Imagine allowing conflict to settle, rather than engaging it—ratcheting up a level, and a level, and a level. Think of the Dalai Lama's soundless smile, Gandhi's quiet walk, Martin Luther King's carefully placed pauses in his stirring orations. Think of anti-war protests where there were songs and speeches, and think of those conducted wholly in silence.

Imagine a nation that listened rather than blogged and posted. A nation that, in times of turmoil, gave itself permission to be still, to *not* speak, not act—until all that was unspoken was given time and space to make its case, to be taken into account.

Imagine that.

"Silence is never really silent," the composer John Cage said.

This I believe.

DIANNE APRILE *is the author and editor of creative nonfiction books. A former journalist and jazz-club co-owner, she is the recipient of fellowships from Kentucky Arts Council, Kentucky Foundation for Women, and Washington state's Artist Trust. Aprile is a member of the nonfiction faculty of Spalding University's brief-residency MFA in writing program. Her latest collaborative project,* The Book, *combines fine-art photographs by Julius Friedman with writers' texts.*

# A Universe on My Shelf

JENNI PADGETT BOHLE

As a child, I lived in a world of history and imagination, emanating from the mustard yellow bookcase that lined the upstairs hallway of my parents' house. The lower shelves contained a full set of navy blue, leather-bound *Encyclopaedia Britannica* with gold lettering, but it was the upper shelves, full of older books that my parents had held onto from college, that fascinated me and made me a book lover. My brother and I were drawn to my dad's Kentucky frontier history book with colorful images of Simon Kenton and Daniel Boone. We were inspired to scout around the pine trees in our front yard as if we were on the lookout for various frontier pitfalls. Because we lived out in the Kentucky countryside, far from suburbia, we used our imaginations to create new worlds, or we adapted our favorite book settings to fit the pond, creeks, and fields on our small farm. Books were what fed our minds and allowed us to see beyond our own limited reality, and the countryside enabled us to create and live, however temporarily, in whatever time or place we could conjure.

My mother's old college literature books were much more daunting because there were no pictures at all, except for the occasional author's portrait (usually a distinguished look-ing man with a formal name like Lord Byron). As a child, I became acquainted with E. E. Cummings, who looked very friendly to me because he didn't capitalize anything, or Lawrence Ferlinghetti, whose *A Coney Island of the Mind* was alluring because the cover was a picture of a blurred amuse-ment park. *Gulliver's Travels* and *Frankenstein* were entire novels I attempted to read because they seemed like cool adventure stories with fascinating covers of monsters and little people. I didn't know it then, but these books and characters were probably responsible for my becoming a college English major many years later.

So I've had a lifelong love affair with books and writ-ing. I believe that Laura Ingalls Wilder and Anne of Green Gables are partially responsible for the feminist I am today, and that without Anne Frank at age 12, I would never have been at all political or interested in human rights. Without Jane Eyre, Elizabeth Bennet, and Catherine Earnshaw, I probably wouldn't have found all-consuming love with my own equivalent to Rochester, Darcy, and Heathcliff.

I believe that when I'm at my lowest, I have only to pick up a Rilke poem or an Emerson essay and I will find some measure of reassurance and guidance. Holden Caulfield's disdain for "phoniness" and Meursault's strength amidst an absurd world sometimes, admittedly, keep me sane. In fact, when I am tempted to shake my head in resignation and disgust at the world, I go back to a timeless and seemingly secret society of writers, poets, and essayists, from Aristotle to Atwood, and I marvel that I belong to this tradition of thoughtful people.

I believe there is a utopia on my bookshelf, and I can be there in an instant. At a time in our culture when appearance and money seem to outweigh anything else, I believe that reading books gives me a sense of where I've come from, and a sense of what it means to be human. And I believe that this plethora of perspectives is among the most vital things we should strive for.

JENNI PADGETT BOHLE *was born and raised on a small farm outside of Perryville, Kentucky, and graduated with a BA from Western Kentucky University and an MA from the University of Kentucky. Currently living in Rheine, Germany, with her husband, she has taught English to political refugees, college freshmen, high school students, and German businesspeople.*

# Serving and Saving Humanity

~

## MOLLY BINGHAM

WHEN YOU ARE SITTING ALONE IN A COLD, DUSTY SIX-BY-
nine-foot concrete prison cell with nothing but a wool
blanket and the constant fear of death, you think. A lot.
You ask yourself questions.

It was March 2003, in the days when Saddam Hussein
still controlled Iraq. I'd been arrested, accused of being a
spy, and was being interrogated and held in solitary con-
finement at Abu Ghraib.

It's one thing to know what you're doing is dangerous
but do it anyway because you think it's right. It is something
else to have your worst fears realized. Would telling this

story of a people during war have an impact? Was it worth the risk? Was it worth prison?

Did I really believe journalism was worth dying for?

I come from a media family. In 1918, my great-grandfather bought the Louisville *Courier-Journal*. My grandfather managed the family companies, as did my father. My family didn't own the paper just because of what it was worth, but because it was worthwhile.

Journalism was considered a public service. A public trust.

Media has a responsibility to inform and educate the community. It plays a critical role in shaping healthy, constructive, and peaceful societies.

Sitting in Abu Ghraib, I knew all of this. The question was, did I really believe it? I did. And I still do. But I also believe media has to change—and change profoundly.

We live in a smaller, more tightly connected world than ever before. We now share across race, religion, and nationality all of our most pressing human concerns and challenges: pandemics, climate change, growing populations, limited resources of food, water, energy. We are one interdependent, global community.

Media hasn't embraced that fact. It doesn't reflect that reality.

We have an opportunity, if not an obligation, to change how media functions and who it's designed to serve. Media is still a public service and a public trust. But the "public" it serves is no longer limited to how far a newspaper can be delivered between rolling off the press and reaching your front door. Media now goes anywhere, anytime. And it must now serve a single, global audience grappling with the challenges of our interdependence.

Media's responsibility is to deliver information relevant to our times and our needs. To deliver information that will help each of us recognize the challenges we share: that we actually have a lot in common, that we share our future.

I know that if we commit to this kind of profound change, if we call for and create a new era of media appropriate to our world, our surroundings, our needs, we will foster a healthy and vibrant community—our global community. We will learn to successfully recognize, understand, and manage our complex and connected world.

So here's what I believe: media not only serving humanity but helping save it.

---

MOLLY BINGHAM *has worked as a photojournalist, journalist, and filmmaker and lives in Washington, DC. Her 2007 film,* Meeting Resistance, *codirected with colleague Steve Connors, tells the story of Iraqi resistance fighters living in Baghdad. Bingham is the founder of ORBmedia (orbmedia.org), a nonprofit organization whose mission is to produce world-class journalism for a global audience that strengthens understanding of our interdependent world.*

# Faith in God and in My Fellow Man

~

## HENRY WARD,
### AS FEATURED IN THE 1950S SERIES

THE MOST IMPORTANT THING IN LIFE, TO ME, IS THE ABILITY to say, with complete sincerity, This I Believe. Life without belief would be a life empty of meaning, dreary and disillusioning. I must have things to believe in and it is most gratifying to me, and my life is made easier, because I have many things in which I do believe.

I believe that there is a certain pattern to life, intricately designed by God, who is just, and so there is no necessity that I understand everything. It is enough that I have faith in the rightness of the pattern that has been set for us. I do not mean by this that I believe my life has been so predes-

tined that there is nothing I can do to influence its course.
If I follow what I know are the proper courses, the inevitable
results that come from rightness will bring fulfillment and
satisfaction to me.

But faith in the rightness of God alone is not enough.
The most miserable man I know is the one who believes
every other man is a liar, and every woman is a cheat. I
must have a measure of faith in my fellow man if I am to
have a full life. A statement made by Vice President Bar-
clay impressed me deeply. "In our form of government," he
said, "the people I have tried to represent have had to put
their trust in me. By the same token, I have had to put my
trust in others." A willingness to put my trust in others is
important to me. I have served with hundreds of persons in
legislative bodies and in governmental offices over a period
of twenty years, and I can count on the fingers of my hands
the ones that I could not trust.

All of my adult life I have been engaged in activities
which have served the public—first as a newspaperman,
then a state legislator, and a public official. I make no claim
that I have dedicated myself to the public good. There has
been satisfaction to me in my activities. But that satisfaction
could not have come if I had not been moved by a deep
conviction that every individual has an inherent right to an
opportunity to earn a richer life.

We like to speak of the right of every person to life, liberty, and the pursuit of happiness. But we delude ourselves if we do not recognize that modern society has made the achievement of that right an uphill battle. Therefore, I find myself cheering when those who struggle and pursue organize themselves to gain their strength through unity. And I have faith in their right to do for themselves, collectively, through their government, what they cannot do for themselves as individuals.

Finally, I honestly believe that honesty is the best policy. There are rewards for the man who does an honest day's work. Honesty pays in business. And sheer, unadulterated honesty in personal dealings will pay dividends. I suppose that I really am saying that I have a high respect for old-fashioned honor. It's a great virtue. All of these things I believe, and I'm glad that I do.

---

HENRY WARD *was born in 1908 in New Hope, Kentucky. He started life as a newspaperman and worked as a cub reporter at the same desk that Irvin S. Cobb had used on the* Paducah News Democrat. *As a Kentucky state representative, senator, and as commissioner of conservation, he took a leading role in the preservation of his native state's natural resources. After suffering defeat in the Kentucky gubernatorial race of 1967, Ward returned to his journalistic career in Paducah until his retirement in 1974. Ward died in 2002.*

# A Nation of Givers

~

## Joseph Smith

IN MY WORK AS A LAW ENFORCEMENT OFFICER, I HAD REGU-
lar contact with the 2 percent of people who commit
murders, extort money, steal goods, rob banks, and prey on
the young and elderly. I came to see these individuals as the
"takers" in our society, and my experiences with them made
me a cynical person.

But twenty-four years ago, my outlook radically changed
and I began to believe in the goodness of people. It happened after a freak accident paralyzed my sixteen-year-old
daughter. She slipped on wet grass while performing a
gymnastic exercise she had done thousands of times. The
accident took my daughter's mobility—or so I thought.

Many friends and neighbors donated time to help our family with the daily chores of mowing grass, cooking meals, and painting as well as modifying my home to make it wheelchair accessible. I had never been on the receiving end of people giving so much, yet wanting nothing in return. As someone who had always depended on myself to provide for my family, I was immensely humbled being ministered to by others.

My daughter's attitude toward life was even more amazing. She graduated from high school a year early and started college. She completed her master's degree in counseling psychology and began working with a humanitarian organization, collecting wheelchairs and medical equipment to be distributed around the world. I have watched as she has traveled extensively over the past few years to Mexico, El Salvador, and Kabul, Afghanistan, delivering supplies to those who have lost hope and dignity.

After several surgeries, my daughter regained the use of both of her arms. She now plays wheelchair tennis and rugby, lives independently, and drives her own van. And she still collects wheelchairs and other equipment to donate to organizations overseas. My daughter has taught me that in spite of setbacks, each person can achieve greatness by looking forward to the possibilities of each new day.

I believe all of us have the potential for greatness every day. As I read the paper each morning and learn of another atrocity or disaster somewhere in the world, I now recognize there are good people there helping their friends and neighbors in their times of need, whether it be the aftermath of hurricanes, auto accidents, kidnappings, bombings, earthquakes, floods, or fires.

Yes, life is still seedy sometimes, but I believe it is also redeeming. We make a conscious choice when we awake each day to become a taker or a giver. I believe our nation will continue to be great because most of us are givers—we truly care for each other in spite of our cultural, ethnic, and religious differences.

---

JOSEPH SMITH *is a retired federal agent. He was inspired by his daughter to complete his doctorate in education. He volunteers at a children's hospital, plays guitar, acts, and is a member of a book club. He lives with his wife in Louisville, Kentucky, and has two grown children and two grandchildren.*

# The Kindnesses We Give Each Other

Mary Popham

KINDNESS IS THE CORNERSTONE OF MY BELIEF. WHEN I GIVE time, attention, or more tangible things to relieve someone's pain or just make their day a little better, then kindnesses are returned to me, magnified and guaranteed. I profit in multiple ways since the things we give away are the very things that remain with us.

Until I was four years old, my parents lived off 31-E, the main highway in Nelson County, Kentucky. Our neighbors across the knob had a daughter named Dorothy, who was four years older than I was. She had a heart condition that prevented her from running and playing like the rest of us. One afternoon, though, Dorothy surprised my siblings and me by offering us piggyback rides, a game we called "horsie." After I watched my younger sister and then my brother trot down the lane and back, Dorothy said to me, "I can't give you a ride. You're too big."

I had eagerly waited for my turn, too young to know that Dorothy had a rheumatic heart and shouldn't have been carrying children on her back. I cried so with heartache that my Aunt Lula, who we called "Ouie," comforted me. "Come into my room. I'm gonna give you a pretty," she said.

Ouie opened a dresser drawer where she kept a box of her favorite things, and from it gave me a little set of plastic bells. The cluster was glued together and had a pin on the back to attach it to a coat or a dress. The set gleamed with bright colors: red, blue, green, and yellow. My disappointment vanished, and I was mesmerized by this gift. I called them my "jingle bells," and I carried them in a special cigar box along with other highly valued items from my childhood: butterfly wings, broken glass in swirling shapes, and unusually colored rocks.

One day, years later, our fifth-grade teacher told the class that a schoolmate's house was on fire. It was the home of Bernadette, the daughter of one of the ladies who cooked in our new lunchroom. When Bernadette began to cry, a wave of sympathy moved me to slip up the aisle to her desk and give her my beloved jingle bells. I wanted her to feel better, but Bernadette didn't even stop crying. As soon as I got back to my desk, I regretted giving away my most precious belonging.

As the years pass, my mind returns occasionally to those two events, the receiving and the giving away of my best treasure. Because my Aunt Lula gave me the jingle bells to soothe my disappointment, and then I gave them to Bernadette to ease her pain, my "little pretty" had taken on magical properties. That feeling of magic remains in my heart today whenever I'm able to give or receive a kindness.

Since earliest childhood, my belief begins and ends with the conviction that we should help each other get through this life, and the method I prefer is by kindness.

*After thirty years of mostly customer service with the GE Company,* MARY POPHAM *retired and obtained an MFA in creative writing from Spalding University. She has published a novel,* Back Home in Landing Run, *and writes book reviews for the* Courier-Journal. *Popham lives with her husband, Ronnie, in Louisville, Kentucky.*

# A Life in Literature

~⌒

## SENA JETER NASLUND

EARLY ON, BY AGE NINE PERHAPS, I DISCOVERED MY PASSION for both reading and writing fiction. The discovery was sudden and unbidden: one very hot summer day in Birmingham (no air conditioning), while reading, I realized I was shivering with cold. I had become caught up in a Laura Ingalls Wilder description of a blizzard. *How is this possible?* I asked myself, and the answer came immediately. *It's these words. Just these words have made me feel cold.* Full of wonder and admiration for Laura's writing, I thought, *I'd like to be able to do that someday.*

Nonetheless, I found myself beginning college as a premed student with the intention of becoming a medical missionary. You see, I wanted to *do good*, or to be a good person, one devoted to the welfare of others. And what of my own love of reading and my interest in imaginative writing? Both still gave me immense pleasure, though I was failing chemistry. *But what good is literature?* I asked myself. And I asked my serious-minded student friends the same question. To spend my life merely doing what I loved seemed unacceptably self-indulgent.

One day in a literature class at my small, excellent liberal arts college, the erudite professor, who was also dean of the college, posed a question that none of us could answer: "In what way are Huck of *Huckleberry Finn* and Pip of Charles Dickens's *Great Expectations* alike?" While I did not know the answer, what I did know—in a strange flash of intuition— was that whatever the answer, it would be of crucial importance to the young man sitting across the aisle from me.

And who was he? A brilliant person, a troubled person for all his brilliance, someone I loved and admired.

The professor answered his own question. "Both are boys in search of a father." And I knew my friend across the aisle, through literature, suddenly understood his own confusion. He knew in a visceral way something of vital importance. What was true of those fictive boys was also true of him: he needed to become a guiding father to himself.

The class was over. As my friend Dwight and I walked out the door together into the hall, he said without looking at me, "And how can you doubt, Sena, that literature can do *good* in the world?" Without looking at him, but sure both his eyes and my eyes were glazed with tears, I replied, "I know. I know." I knew that literature could and does make ideas and feelings real, dramatic, and accessible in a way that enhances the quality of our lives.

And so I gave myself permission to embrace a literary life, both as reader and as writer. If something I might come to write offered one wonderful person a new and needed perspective, then I could justify choosing a life for myself in literature.

That was all a very long time ago, about half a century ago. My friend would die in an auto accident before he was twenty-one. And I would live to be extraordinarily happy in my choice of professions.

This I believe: that the arts must be a part of education at all levels, that the arts can and do offer us not only pleasure but also invaluable insights into ourselves and our world.

SENA JETER NASLUND *is the author of nine works of fiction,
including* Ahab's Wife; Four Spirits; Abundance, a Novel
of Marie Antoinette; Adam & Eve; *and* The Foun-
tain of St. James Court; or, Portrait of the Artist as an
Old Woman. *She was Kentucky Poet Laureate 2005–2006
and received the Alabama Governor's Award in the Arts in 2011.
Winner of the Harper Lee Prize for Distinguished Writing, she is
program director and co-founder of the Spalding University brief-
residency MFA in writing and writer in residence at the University
of Louisville.*

*They Lived Their Faith*

⌒

## CHARLES HENRY PARRISH,
### AS FEATURED IN THE 1950S SERIES

As I LOOK BACK, I HAVE THE GROWING CONVICTION THAT
much of what I now believe may be traced to my parents. My
present attitudes seem to have resulted from an accumulation of many small and apparently insignificant childhood
experiences. These beliefs I hold must have taken root early
because as far back as I can remember, they were no different fundamentally from what they are now.

As the son of a Baptist minister, I have often wondered
why my religious beliefs were not more strictly orthodox.
Undoubtedly it was the sort of person my father was, rather
than what he said in sermons or pamphlets, that influenced

me most. My father's private secretary was Catholic. It never seemed incongruous to me that he should bring back to her beads that had been blessed by Pope Pius X or that a large picture of the pope should be prominently displayed in our home. Because of this memory, perhaps, the theological technicalities of doctrinal disputes leave me completely unmoved. I believe that every man must find God for himself, and that it does not really matter under whose auspices the search is made.

Nearly always, as I can remember, there were non-paying guests at our house. Uncomplainingly, my mother would do the necessary things to make them comfortable. Sometimes the persons who came were complete strangers. A gospel singer who had missed her train called up from the station and asked to be put up for the night. She stayed for three weeks. A stranded evangelist was with us for all of one winter. I do not recall that anyone was ever turned away. People in trouble inevitably came to my father for help. Although victimized many times, he was always ready to do whatever he could for the next person who asked his aid. He seemed not to think of himself. Yet, he enjoyed a moderate prosperity and his family never wanted for anything. It has thus become a part of me to believe that in the long run, I could never lose anything by helping other people.

The details of my father's early life have always been a source of inspiration for me. It was a life of struggle. To the ordinary difficulties encountered was added the handicap of his racial origin. He had to fight continuously against racial intolerance. What has become increasingly significant for me was that he fought without bitterness. So far as I know, he never hated anybody. He must have believed in the essential goodness of people. I have come, gradually, to share this belief.

If I have stressed the importance of my father in determining my basic outlook on life, it is not to leave the impression that the influence of my mother has been negligible. It is, rather, that they were of one mind on the fundamental issues. My mother had varied outside interests, too, but her own family was the center of her loyalties. No sacrifice was too great for those she loved. Her devotion has had a profound influence in shaping my evaluations and beliefs.

These memories and impressions of my parents are the materials out of which my credo has been forged. Perhaps they would not have phrased it as I have. They might not have put it into words at all. They lived their faith. Its essence for me is couched on the belief that if I look always for the good in other people, I will surely catch a vision of God.

*As a professor of sociology at the University of Louisville, DR. CHARLES HENRY PARRISH, born in 1899 in Louisville, was the first African-American to be appointed to the faculty of a public Southern (and predominantly white) university. Parrish chaired U of L's Department of Sociology from 1959 to 1964 and was invited to the inauguration of President Lyndon B. Johnson in 1965. Parrish retired from teaching in 1969 and died at his daughter's home in Newark, New Jersey, in 1989.*

# Prayer Is All There Is

~

## Tammy Ruggles

I BELIEVE IN THE POWER OF PRAYER. THE BIBLE SAYS TO train up a child in the way that he should go, and in the end he will not depart from it.

I hung all of my hopes and prayers on that one verse for my only child, a son, conceived in love with my teenage sweetheart. My boyfriend was a playful ruffian who grew into a troubled man who battled alcohol and demons. He wound up in prison while I ended up in a college classroom. Two weeks after he was released from prison at age thirty-nine, he died in an automobile accident.

Our twenty-year, up-and-down relationship bore one good thing, one lasting symbol, and that was our beautiful son. While the man I loved was locked behind bars for ten years for burglary, I prayed night and day for our son. I prayed that he would stay clean and sober, walk the straight and narrow, do right instead of wrong, and be a good man.

I prayed this prayer almost every day and every night. Sometimes more than once a day. Sometimes with every breath I breathed. I tried to be the good example, the good mentor, the good parent. I stopped smoking, I didn't drink, I didn't swear, I took him to church. I had lots of long talks with him about life's challenges. Yet my fear that my son might end up like his father consumed me. My heart lurched every time he left to hang out with his teenage friends.

Prayer by prayer, day by day, tear by tear, we made it through his adolescence. He had his ups and downs, a few close calls, a night or two in jail for drinking, but nothing too serious. Nothing too irreparable.

At twenty-one, my son is already a better man, a more productive and thoughtful man, than his father was. He is a carpenter's apprentice, choosing to build things up instead of tearing them down, doing something good, instead of bad, with his hands. His father had already been to prison by the time he was twenty-one. My son has more than a fighting chance.

I realize God doesn't respond to every prayer the way we want or hope. I prayed my heart out for my boy's dad, and I felt like that prayer went unanswered. I can only say that my son turning onto the right path almost makes up for that seemingly unanswered prayer. So I thank God every day that He has kept my son from fulfilling my worst nightmare. My son, unfairly, has a lot to live down and a lot to make up for. He carries his father's reputation with him wherever he goes, and I know people can see it on him like a badge.

I just wonder if they ever see me in him.

I still pray that prayer. I still have faith in it. I still believe it.

---

TAMMY RUGGLES *is a legally blind finger painter and writer based in Kentucky. Her writing credits include a paperback book,* Peace, *published by Clear Light Books in 2005;* Chicken Soup For the Soul; *Disney's* Family Fun Magazine; Spirituality and Health; A Cup of Comfort; *and many others. Family, faith, and friends are very important parts of her life.*

# We Need a Revolution

$\backsim$

## Carol Besse

I BELIEVE IN REVOLUTION. AND REVOLUTION IS EXACTLY what we need in this country—and we need it now.

I am a child of the '60s, so I grew up in the midst of a revolution. One of the first things I did when I left home for college was to join every anti-war protest I could find. Never one described as cautious or timid, I loved to be in the midst of a loud and raucous group trying to right a wrong.

And today my friends often hear me ask, sometimes at the top of my voice, "Why in the heck aren't we out marching in the streets today—and tomorrow and every day?"

And exactly what are we to rebel against? The list is

practically endless—the destruction of our environment, the takeover of our government by special interests, the meltdown of our economy, the growing inequity in our society—everywhere that entrenched corporate and political interests have a chokehold on our culture. Insurance companies tell us we can't have national health care; oil and auto industries tell us we can't have fuel-efficient, clean cars; politicians tell us we can't have a government uncorrupted by money. But we must have these things.

We need a revolution, but it's not really a revolution until someone gets hurt. We need some pain, and we need everyone to feel it. Too often the pain is borne by those least able to bear it. Four-dollar-a-gallon gas is painful, but it may take $10- or $20-a-gallon gas before the outrage of the people is loud enough and menacing enough to rock our complacency. We've been asleep at the wheel for too long now, and the car is out of control, headed toward the cliff.

There are two things that I am passionate about—books and birds—and both are threatened with extinction if we don't change our course and change it fast. Reading is what I do to connect with the world outside myself, but it's also how I learned almost everything I know. We have already begun to see the disastrous effects of the decline in reading and literacy. If people stop reading they are at the mercy of politicians and marketers and corporate hucksters of every sort. An uninformed populace is our greatest danger.

My second great passion is birds—birding is how I connect with the natural world, with my planet, our planet. And I see an even more precipitous decline in the health and viability of our ecosystems than I do in reading. Our environment is nearing a tipping point from which we'll not be able to recover. And if the planet is lost, none of the rest really matters, does it? If the planet is lost, then it seems foolish to speak of half-measures, to take small steps, to talk about going slow.

We need a revolution. This I believe.

CAROL BESSE *is the co-owner of Carmichael's Bookstore in Louisville, Kentucky, which was named* Publishers Weekly *bookseller of the year in 2009. A native of New Hampshire, Besse moved to Louisville in 1978. She is an avid birdwatcher and an advocate of supporting local businesses.*

# Innocence Is Overrated

MARY ANN JOHNSON

ON ONE OF THOSE SPECIAL DAYS WHEN MY OLDEST DAUGH-
ter was about eighteen, we had a heart-to-heart conversation.
She told me, "You said something once which really made
sense."

I was surprised I had ever said anything worth remembering. Hey, I actually said something she remembered! I
wondered which of my words had stuck with her. I was
expecting something profound, something I had tossed out
in a moment of unconscious genius.

"You said, 'Innocence is overrated.'"

"Oh," I said slowly. Out of all the advice, the hints,
the suggestions I had given her over the years, she picked

this one to emulate. Oh my God, what would my mother have thought? The world I grew up in revered innocence. I was sure my mother was turning in her grave at that very moment.

Innocence is overrated. I vaguely remembered saying this to her but couldn't remember why. I think it was one of those flippant remarks I made one day out of frustration when talking about one of her friends' conservative family. Innocence is overrated.

Well, innocence *is* overrated. After all, what is innocence but a lack of knowledge? Babies arrive in this world in innocence and we try our best to keep them innocent as long as possible, but at what price to them? As children grow, we protect them, but at some point this becomes detrimental to their development. How can we expect them to learn how to deal with the real world if they are kept from it? Perhaps I feel this way because I was raised in that mode. I remember the struggles I had when confronted with new situations for which I was not prepared.

One can never anticipate every aspect of what the world will reveal to your children. When my youngest daughter was about ten, she typed "girls.com" on our computer, thinking she would find a website with jewelry, makeup, and other things for girls. However, when she hit "enter," well, you can imagine what she saw. When I discovered this, I was not angry, nor did I put parental controls on the computer. We talked about what she had seen, why some people go to these sites, and how to use search engines. Evidently I laughed, though I don't remember it that way. She says I did.

But the point is that I helped her deal with the situation rather than making her feel afraid of it. I believe that can work whether discussing politics, controversial art, movies, discrimination, or any number of other things.

I don't propose that we force children to lose their innocence. But an innocent young adult is naïve, and naïveté does not help a person think clearly or solve problems.

So I do believe innocence is overrated. I believe in curiosity. I believe in answering questions. I believe in respecting children and their rights to grow into thoughtful, worldly adults who can make their own decisions based on fact and not fear.

---

*After working as a nurse and wound-care specialist for over thirty years, MARY ANN JOHNSON has shed that role to become a full-time grandmother, traveler, and lover of life. She will soon be moving from Kentucky to Fairfax, Virginia, to live with her daughter, son-in-law, and three granddaughters.*

# Turning 'Til We Come Round Right

～

## Dee Wade

My wife, son, and I spent one summer day a few years ago paddling down the Green River through the heart of Kentucky. We were joined by many companions. There were people fishing at bridges and roadsides, and we were also joined by the fish they weren't catching. Above, there were more species of birds than we could name.

We identify four snakes, scads of turtles, three beavers, one presumably drowned groundhog, butterflies galore, a family of deer, and later, near dusk, a wild turkey and a red fox. It's as if all things living—and one dead—decide to show up and march in our parade.

At one point, resting, I lean back in the kayak, eyes heavenward. High above flies a jetliner, a tiny silver toy against a field of blue. So they, the passengers, are with us, too, though they probably don't see us. Like us, they are in transit from here to there, between ascent and descent, including the woman in 16B who just nodded off, book in lap. We are, quite literally, on two different planes of existence—we who float on watery currents, and they who speed through streams of air.

Yet we share the same life, along with the birds and fish and mammals and butterflies. I believe each life is remembered by a personal Being who makes us and keeps us in mind. Everything is noted, nothing missed, from the acrobatics of the Prothonotary Warbler we just passed, the dreams of the woman up in 16B, and that star that just winked out three galaxies away. How all that happens I cannot imagine. But it certainly deepens the mystery of the Source of All Being and therefore life's destiny.

Holy warriors would divide us between the infidel and the righteous, saved and unsaved. They know not what they do. We are one human race, because that's the nature of things. Of this I am certain: relationship radiates from the center of the universe because its Creator chose connection in the beginning. By definition, relationship is not static but dynamic and free, sometimes messy, always evolving. Relationship is richer than a parade; it's a dance.

Perhaps the woman aloft in 16B is in the National Guard,

on her way to Iraq. Whether she is misled into another war of aggression or not, we rightly honor her sacrifice, and especially that of the fallen. I believe this personal Being—whom I call God—remembers them all, the dead American and the dead Iraqi, for it is by God's initiative, not ours, that the living earth abounds in wondrous variety, and God remembers God's own.

And so it is on the occasion of this summer day past that I am reminded that we are all related. I believe we need to get together and practice our dance steps: alabam' left, swing your partner. Creation itself has interest in our choreography. And even God—the original dancer—waits for us to step, slide, step, to do-si-do, to turn, turn, till by turning, turning, we come 'round right.

DEE WADE *is from both Hodgenville and Campbellsville, Kentucky, and he is currently pastor of Anchorage Presbyterian Church in Anchorage. Mr. Wade is married to Deborah Newton Wade, a social worker, and they have one son, Seth. Mr. Wade graduated from the University of Kentucky in 1974 and from Union Theological Seminary in New York City in 1978.*

# Service to Others Pays Big Dividends

~⌐

## SIDNEY ROSENBLUM,
### AS FEATURED IN THE 1950S SERIES

I WAS BORN AND BROUGHT UP IN A SMALL COUNTRY TOWN OF about 1,500 population. I am of the firm belief that I enjoyed advantages of down-to-earth community feelings, friendships, and even obligations that a large city does not offer. My mother used to remind me that everyone in our town was our friend and that we were to respect them and always to remember that there was good in everyone. I soon learned that our citizens were judged for what they do, more than for who they are.

My parents were foreign-born, and when they settled in the little community of Springfield, Tennessee, in the early

1880s, they were the only family of Jewish faith there. But the matter of religion made little difference since friends were made and cultivated through interests, age groups, and the usual likes and dislikes. People were just concerned with the welfare of their neighbors, and they were quick to be helpful whenever the occasion arose. How well I can recollect that when Sundays came along, my mother used to say, "Go to church with the boys and girls. It's much better than associating with those who keep away from churches."

There were no automobiles or bus travel in those days, and we had to take the train for Nashville, Tennessee, to attend services of our faith. We always did this on the high holidays. How could I help but believe that every person was born with good in him, and even though it may be hard to bring out the good in a small percentage of individuals, it certainly is there, and one should not be too quick to condemn or criticize. I grew to understand that it did not take wealth or success or creed or color to make friends. Today, I firmly believe that friendship is one of my life's most precious assets.

I had become of teen age when we moved to Louisville, Kentucky, which is still my home. It was here, in 1919, that our present business was organized by my father, my two brothers, and myself. As our business grew it became possible for me to give more time to outside activities. I became a member of the Rotary Club, the motto of which is "Service Above Self." I began to realize, more than ever, that even after my early teachings, I had not put enough effort into the needs of others. I was appointed a member of the Rotary Crippled Children's Committee, the work of which I soon learned was of great interest and appeal. I began to see the good that could be done for others less fortunate than I and, comparatively speaking, with little time and effort on my part, but with a measurable benefit to others, and satisfaction and contentment to me in return.

This all led to my interest in the Boy Scout organization and their program of building citizens of tomorrow, and ultimately to the fine work being done for others by the Salvation Army. I found myself spending more and more time in civic and communal affairs, which resulted in a different kind of dividend—in many ways more pleasant than clipping an interest-bearing coupon. I suppose that as one grows older, the satisfaction of aiding others becomes greater.

Finally, I cannot help but believe that life is really what I put into it, and that if I were but determined to give thought and consideration to others and to remember that all men are born free and equal, I will derive a pleasure and a keen and indescribable gratification that one can get in no other way.

Born in 1897 in Tennessee, SIDNEY ROSENBLUM was executive vice president of the Enro Shirt Company in Louisville, Kentucky. He founded the business with his father and two brothers in 1919, and was active in Louisville industry and civic affairs from then on. Rosenblum served as the director of the Kentucky Society for Crippled Children, which he headed for twenty-four years. Rosenblum died in 1961.

# Reverence for the Twelve O'Clock Whistle

—&#8765;

## Joy Moore

I'VE BEEN ENAMORED BY LIFE SINCE 1978. I WAS ALMOST born in the backseat of a '73 Grand Torino, barreling down River Road in Estill County, Kentucky. I had crowned amid prayers to Jesus spoken in tongues and the squeaking jack hoisting the tail end of the car up so my father could change the flat tire. The spare was bald, too. There between the river and train track was almost I. Life for me has always had a way of holding itself in, until now.

I believe in the inner voice and how it can resonate, resilient. Growing up poor was necessary for me to know what cracks to not fall into. It set the tone for my life. Poverty was a blessing, in retrospect. It forced me to use my imagination. I could hear the tune of a thousand songs as my Aunt Ruby strummed an old two-stringed guitar. I could build a fortress with the scrap wood blocks Daddy would bring in to stoke the stove in winter. I could sail the high seas as I sat beneath the sheets my mother would hang out on the line. I felt them wisp and snap about me in summer heat storms. I could ride my bicycle to the end of a world that rested on the rim of where gravel meets blacktop.

I believe in the land and how it gives eagerly, despite. There were years when the harvest seemed like manna. Plums so ripe and heavy they split the limbs from the trees. Walnuts that turned our fingertips green. Blackberries by the gallon buckets. The stringing and snapping of beans on the front porch from the twelve o'clock whistle until the sun went down, for days. All abundant from the prayers, the rain, and the drawing of water from the well. Every living thing thrived from the love in and around home.

I believe in being lighthearted and good-natured. In laughing so hard, you cry. In counting your blessings instead of your money. In remembering where you came from.

I am thankful that I was forged with inner and outer peace. I am thankful for a childhood filled with the beautiful, simple, plain old everyday. I believe in that extraordinary love, so powerful that it still echoes and resounds within me, giving light to a world so full of dark moments.

JOY MOORE *is one of those Slabtown Moores known for turning phrases. She holds a master's degree in interdisciplinary social science from Morehead State University.*

# *Finding Home*

❧

## Anna Whites

My mother was a traveler. We lived on three continents by the time I was five. She searched for meaning and art and experiences. I wanted a hearth like those in storybooks, with rocks stacked by great-grandfathers and firewood from trees planted by an ancestor. I looked for my home in London, where the weight of history made pieces of brick crumble into the street. I searched for home in Kenya, under a sky so flat it seemed to go on forever, baking the trays of tiny fish that grandmothers fed the babies who were strapped to their hips. I asked the sawgrass of Florida and the lush green leaves of Madrone trees in California, "Are you what home looks like?"

When I met my husband he told me not to marry him unless I was willing to move to eastern Kentucky, back to where his grandmothers lived. The first two years were hard. I was an outsider, classified by all who met me as "not from here." I would come home each evening and complain about standing in line at the grocery store while the clerk chatted aimlessly with the customer in front of me about church news and the health of neighbors.

One day, while registering the car at the courthouse, I was sharing stories with the woman next to me when I suddenly noticed the irritated face of someone "not from here" standing behind us. In that very moment, I realized that I was no longer the outsider—I am from here. That small town had woven me into the daily pattern of its life without me even noticing. My neighbors were my friends. My husband's grandmother was my Maw-Maw. My children walked the streets where their father grew up and sat on church pews emblazoned with their grandfather's initials.

But it wasn't just that which made it home. It was how connected I felt to the courage of the women who made beautiful quilts out of hand-me-down rags . . . the fierce pride of those who survived hardship for generations and had the stories to prove it . . . the humor of people who came through the worst, decade after decade, and still thought life was pretty darn funny . . . and the way they reached out to me and made me whole. And did I mention that my home is beautiful? That there is nothing more gorgeous than the speed with which black velvet evening covers the hills? Nothing more magical than dew glowing on redbud branches or ice sparkling on limbs dipping into the creek?

I believe we all need somewhere to call home. I've found that home isn't just a place; it's where I feel I belong.

I don't live in Louisa right now, having traded a small town for the state capital and blue jeans for suits, at least temporarily. But it's still my home—so much so that when I drive up the interstate and come around the curve leading to the first of the hills marking eastern Kentucky, I can't breathe for all the happiness that wells up in my heart. I may still be a traveler, but now I know I have a home. No matter what, I can walk in the door of the Lawrence County courthouse, tomorrow or twenty years from now, and we will pick up talking about the news of the day as if I'd never left.

ANNA WHITES *is an attorney in Frankfort, Kentucky, practicing health and education law. She is the president of the Board of the Maker's Mark Secretariat Center, which retrains retired racehorses, and she is a member of the Interagency Commission on Autism Spectrum Disorders. She is married to Pierce Whites, and they have a daughter, Amanda, who is a ballerina, and a son, Lawson, who is a Mandarin Chinese translator.*

# *Appendix*

~~~

## HOW TO WRITE YOUR OWN
## THIS I BELIEVE ESSAY

WE INVITE YOU TO CONTRIBUTE TO THIS PROJECT BY WRITing and submitting your own statement of personal belief. We understand how challenging this is—it requires intense self-examination, and many find it difficult to begin. To guide you through this process, we offer these suggestions:

**Tell a story:** Be specific. Take your belief out of the ether and ground it in the events that have shaped your core values. Think of your own experience, work, and family, and tell of the things you know that no one else does. Your story need not be heart-warming or gut-wrenching—it can even be funny—but it should be *real* and it should be about

199

*you*. Consider moments when belief was formed or tested or changed. Make sure your story ties to the essence of your daily life philosophy and the shaping of your beliefs.

**Be brief:** Your statement should be between 500 and 600 words. The shorter length forces you to focus on one belief that is central to your life.

**Name your belief:** If you can't name it in a sentence or two, your essay might not be about belief. Also, rather than writing a list, consider focusing on one core belief.

**Be positive:** Say what you do believe, not what you don't believe. Avoid statements of religious dogma, preaching, or editorializing.

**Be personal:** Make your essay about you; speak in the first person. Avoid speaking in the editorial "we." Write in words and phrases that are comfortable for you to speak. We recommend that you read your essay aloud to yourself several times, and each time edit it and simplify it until you find the words, tone, and story that truly echo your belief and the way you speak.

Please submit your completed essay to the This I Believe project by visiting the website, www.thisibelieve.org.

# Acknowledgments

WE MUST FIRST OFFER DEEP AND HEARTFELT GRATITUDE TO all the essayists who contributed their work to this book. We are ever thankful for their willingness to say "yes" to expressing the things that matter most and for sharing their stories in this collection.

Since reviving This I Believe in 2004, we have enjoyed continued and hearty support from Casey Murrow, Keith Wheelock, and Margot Wheelock Schlegel, the children of the *This I Believe* radio program creators Edward R. Murrow and Ward Wheelock. We remain grateful for their encouragement of our stewardship of their parents' powerful idea. Our project continues to be guided by Edward R. Murrow and his team, which preceded us in the 1950s: Gladys Chang Hardy, Reny Hill, Donald J. Merwin, Edward P. Morgan, Raymond Swing, and Ward Wheelock.

We're truly grateful to John Gregory for his longtime collaborative work as editor and producer at This I Believe and specifically for his expert editing in this volume.

We offer our sincere thanks to Julia Steiner, intern extraordinaire. Her assistance was much appreciated, and her talents are immeasurable.

We thank Henry Holt and Company for use of the essay "Creative Solutions to Life's Challenges," Copyright ©2005 by Frank X Walker. From the book *This I Believe: The Personal Philosophies of Remarkable Men and Women*, edited by Jay Allison and Dan Gediman. Copyright ©2006 by This I Believe, Inc. Reprinted with permission from Henry Holt and Company, LLC.

We would also like to thank John Wiley & Sons for use of the following essays, which are reprinted here with their permission:

"Important Strangers," Copyright ©2011 by Leslie Guttman. From the book *This I Believe: Life Lessons*, edited by Dan Gediman. Copyright ©2011 by This I Believe, Inc.

"Dancing to the Music," Copyright ©2012 by Amanda Joseph-Anderson. From the book *This I Believe: On Motherhood*, edited by Dan Gediman. Copyright ©2012 by This I Believe, Inc.

"A Lesson I Hold Dear," Copyright ©2011 by Kara Gebhart Uhl. From the book *This I Believe: Life Lessons*, edited by Dan Gediman. Copyright ©2011 by This I Believe, Inc.

"The Power of Parenthood," Copyright ©2012 by Andrea Coleman. From the book *This I Believe: On Mother-*

*hood*, edited by Dan Gediman. Copyright ©2012 by This I Believe, Inc.

Special thanks go to Jay Allison and Viki Merrick at Atlantic Public Media in Woods Hole, Massachusetts, for editing and producing for radio the essays "Creative Solutions to Life's Challenges" and "I Am Still 'The Greatest.'"

Our deepest and sincerest thanks go to our This I Believe, Inc., board of directors, who give their time and talents to strengthening our organization. Thank you to Martin J. Bollinger, Patti Magers, William E. May, Steve Ramsay, Randy Ratliff, Keith Runyon, and Jodi Skees. A special word of thanks to Keith for penning the Introduction to this volume.

We would also like to thank the following people who opened doors for us or otherwise helped this book be successful: Ina Brown Bond, Christy Brown, Gill Holland, Eleanor Bingham Miller, Al Shands, Jackie Howard, and Karen Mann.

Our current on-air home is the *Bob Edwards Show* on Sirius XM Satellite Radio and *Bob Edwards Weekend* on Public Radio International. We have the continued good fortune of working with Bob Edwards and his wonderful staff each week: Steve Lickteig, Geoffrey Redick, Ed McNulty, Ariana Pekary, Shelley Tillman, Dan Bloom, Andy Kubis, Chad Campbell, and Cristy Meiners. At Sirius XM, we thank Jeremy Coleman, Frank Raphael, and Kevin Straley.

# ACKNOWLEDGMENTS

The creation of this book would not have been possible without the support and encouragement of Carol Butler at Butler Books. We are so fortunate to have her in our corner. In addition, we are thankful for the talents of Susan Salsburg, Eric Butler, and Scott Stortz, who worked hard to make this book the quality publication that it is.

And, finally, we thank the tens of thousands of individuals who have accepted our invitation to write and share their own statements of belief. This book holds only a fraction of the many thoughtful and inspiring essays that have been submitted to our project, and we are grateful for them all. We invite you to join this group by writing your own This I Believe essay and submitting it to us via our website, www.thisibelieve.org. You will find instructions in the appendix of this book on how to do so.